# CLASSIC
# CARVING
# PATTERNS

# CLASSIC
# CARVING
# PATTERNS

LORA S. IRISH

The Taunton Press

COVER PHOTO: Scott Phillips

Printed in the United States of America
10 9 8 7 6 5 4 3 2 1

*Classic Carving Patterns* was originally published in hardcover
© 1997 by The Taunton Press, Inc.

The Taunton Press, 63 South Main Street, PO Box 5506,
Newtown, CT 06470-5506
e-mail: tp@taunton.com

Distributed by Publishers Group West

Library of Congress Cataloging-in-Publication Data

Irish, Lora S.
    Classic carving patterns / Lora S. Irish.
      p.   cm.
    "A Fine woodworking book" — T.p. verso.
    ISBN 1-56158-173-9 hardcover
    ISBN 1-56158-318-9 softcover
    1. Wood-carving — Patterns.    I. Title.
TT199.7.I75   1997
736'.4 — dc21                                96-46958
                                                CIP

**About Your Safety**
Working wood is inherently dangerous. Using hand or power tools improperly or
ignoring standard safety practices can lead to permanent injury or even death. Don't try
to perform operations you learn about here (or elsewhere) unless you're certain they are
safe for you. If something about an operation doesn't feel right, don't do it. Look for
another way. We want you to enjoy the craft, so please keep safety foremost in your mind
whenever you're in the shop.

# CONTENTS

*In memory of my father,*

**H. Ralph Cunningham
(1924–1995),**

*an old whittler
from way back*

# INTRODUCTION

As a freelance artist, I've always felt it important to keep a file of designs and project ideas that I've completed. This file, or artist's morgue, is a record of work that I've done as well as a source of reference that I can draw on for future works. When I began carving wood several years ago, it was natural to start compiling a file of patterns specifically for woodworking. As with most craftspeople, one idea often creates several variations and those variations expand into new ideas. This book is a sampling of those ideas.

You will find within these pages detailed drawings of patterns made for wood, which you can use for carving, burning, or painting. The detailed pencil sketches will help you visualize the final dimensions of your carving or the shading line of your painting. With each drawing, there's a larger outline pattern of the design that you can use for transferring to your own project. (Depending on the scale at which you're working, you can use the patterns at the size shown or enlarge or reduce them on a copier.) Although the designs are clearly created, it will be your imagination that will transform them into fine furniture and other heirloom creations.

Many of the designs contain reference marks that will direct you in squaring the pattern to your work or a center mark for compass placement on circular designs. Also included at the end of the book are a few tips on pattern making and design transfer.

Whether you're looking for a small accent or a large panel pattern, a corner or a curve, I hope that this book will help to spark your imagination.

# 1

# PATTERN THEMES & SHAPES

Throughout history, carving patterns have tended to follow a group of general themes. These themes include geometric and repetitive pattern themes, natural pattern themes, the human form and face, fantasy pattern themes, and storytelling pattern themes.

## GEOMETRIC AND REPETITIVE PATTERN THEMES

Some of the earliest designs that artists created were based on repeating circles and spirals, chevrons, and line work. The simplicity of a banded line or a beaded edge is still used today as a primary accent to furniture making. Repetitive lines and geometric patterns establish a rhythm throughout the entire form. The skilled use of a routed edge or a fine inlaid line of contrasting wood can transform a simple furniture

design into a classic work of art. Chip carving is a wonderful example of the use of repetitive pattern. Basic triangles magically transform into elaborate circles, diamonds, and squares that capture the viewer's attention with their depth and highlights.

By creating a single unit of work and carrying that design throughout the form, you can capture the interest of the viewer. This style of artwork is very simplistic, and each area of enhancement is predictable. Just as it is obvious that glassware of different sizes but with a repetitive design belongs together, we can expect that furniture with a repetitive theme will be used together in the same setting. When a piece of furniture is designed with two different elements, such as a bookcase mounted on a desk, a repetitive design unites the elements into one complete piece.

REPETITIVE GEOMETRIC PATTERN
*(see p. 21)*

NATURAL THISTLE
PATTERN *(see p. 17)*

of simple flowers that often includes violets, pansies, daisies, and wild roses, reflects the trend toward English-style flower gardens during the late 1800s. The acanthus-leaf pattern became popular during the 1600s and is still a classic carving theme today because of its flowing, expressive lines, its simplicity in carving, and its adaptability to different elements of furniture.

The hex sign and the distelfink pattern can quickly be dated to the 18th- and 19th-century Pennsylvania Dutch. Today this simple form of art has found new popularity in modern stencil work and primitive landscapes used on refinished furniture.

Natural themes may either be true to nature, as in modern decoy-carving work where each feather is carefully and accurately placed, or stylized, as in antique decoy work where only the most general impression of the form is carved. Both create decoys, yet each has its own feel and form.

## NATURAL PATTERN THEMES

The second general theme area for the carver is natural images. Leaves and flowers, birds and animals, and landscapes are everyday images that appear in ornamentation. Given that nature allows the artist the widest range of ideas, it is not surprising that this is the largest category of design themes.

Natural artwork often identifies the region where the art was created. The thistle design is commonly associated with artwork from Scotland, while the cherry-blossom design is traditionally Japanese. The eagle and star pattern quickly brings the viewer to the American shores. Artists from different regions may even treat their interpretation of a design idea differently. An English artist may create a rose as a multipetaled semicircular flower with a simple center, whereas an American artist may draw the rose as a tightly wrapped cylinder with a few escaping petals.

Not only does the natural pattern help to establish where the art was made, but it can also identify when it was created. The nosegay pattern, a circular cluster

## HUMAN FORM AND FACE

Carvers have used the human form and face as a theme to reflect both mankind's ideas and emotions. In ornamentation, the human face, often male, can take on physical attributes from nature. Ram's and bull's horns lend a mythical, powerful feeling to the design. Hair, mustaches, and beards flow and interweave with leaves and branches to represent the

MYTHICAL HUMAN FACE *(see p. 150)*

FANTASY PATTERN *(see p. 143)*

mystery of nature. Angel wings and halos can lift the viewer to Heaven, while deer antlers and lion fangs added to a face show us man's darker side. Whereas geometric patterns and natural patterns allow carvers to deal with recognizable shapes or to copy the real world around them, patterns in the human form and face category encourage artists to explore mankind's fascination with nature.

## FANTASY PATTERN THEMES

Fantasy images are often used to capture the unexplainable events or fears of daily life. Gargoyles, winged dragons, devils, and angels all show up on the carver's palette of ideas. Eastern dragons portend cataclysmic natural events, such as volcanic eruptions and earthquakes, but they can also be representative of good omens. During the Middle Ages, Western dragons represented man's dark side. Today, dragons show the mythical and fanciful nature of man.

Gargoyles are often the artist's way of poking fun at his fellow man. Here the carver can create a distinct impression in the viewer by exaggerating physical features and emphasizing emotional expression. Even though the gargoyle design appears to be a mythical animal, gargoyles are commonly shown in human poses doing human tasks.

## STORYTELLING PATTERN THEMES

Many designs are used to tell visual stories. Scenes that include a retriever, quail, and pastoral background relate a tale about the excitement of the hunt. A country scene created with an old farmhouse and decaying barn may tell a story about the carver's feelings of home and roots. By using storytelling themes the artist can record man's daily life and activities. Each element of the story becomes united within the boundaries of the relief. Historically, storytelling themes have appeared in every area of artwork, from

STORYTELLING PATTERN *(see p. 146)*

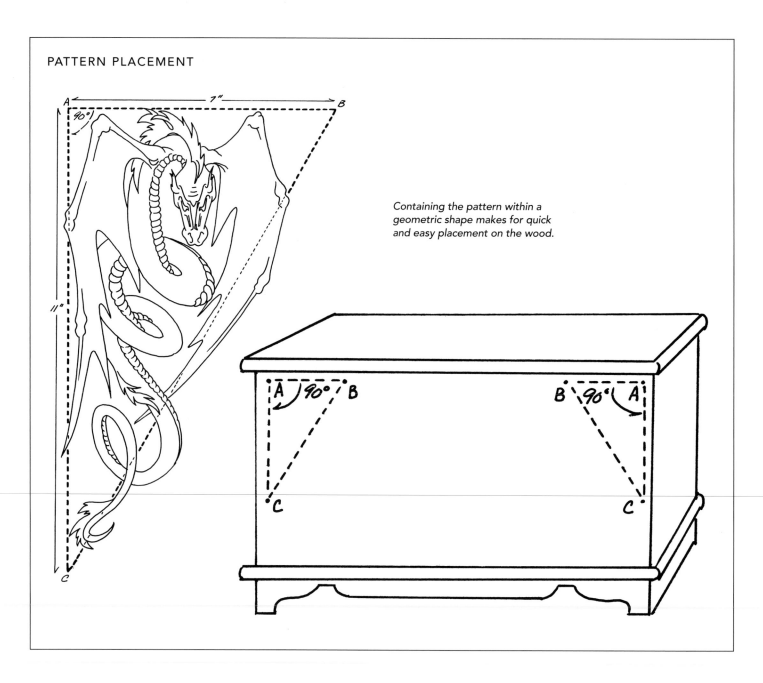

Containing the pattern within a geometric shape makes for quick and easy placement on the wood.

fresco and mosaic murals to small jewelry box lids. This pattern theme has a strong place in today's wood crafting, as reflected in the marvelous relief carvings and wood burnings that are currently being done.

## BASIC DESIGN SHAPES

Many of the patterns used for wood carving, burning, and painting are free-flowing designs with branches, leaves, and floral accents. Planning the placement of these patterns on the wood can be difficult since there are few reference points that relate to the structure of the furniture. Establishing a general shape to the design, or determining the general area that the design will use, can make the planning of the final project easier. Because a triangle has three straight sides and three definite angles it is easier to measure and place on the wood to be carved than a design of a dragon that has no definite or measurable boundaries. But if the dragon design can be contained in the general outline of a triangle and the triangle is used for placement marks, the dragon design can be readily transferred to the wood (see the drawing above).

Most designs fall into one of seven basic shapes: line, triangle, square and rectangle, circle and oval, S-curve and C-curve, mirror image, and free-form. All of these basic design shapes make use of lines, angles, and points that can be measured and easily transferred to the wood (see the drawing on the facing page).

## BASIC DESIGN SHAPES

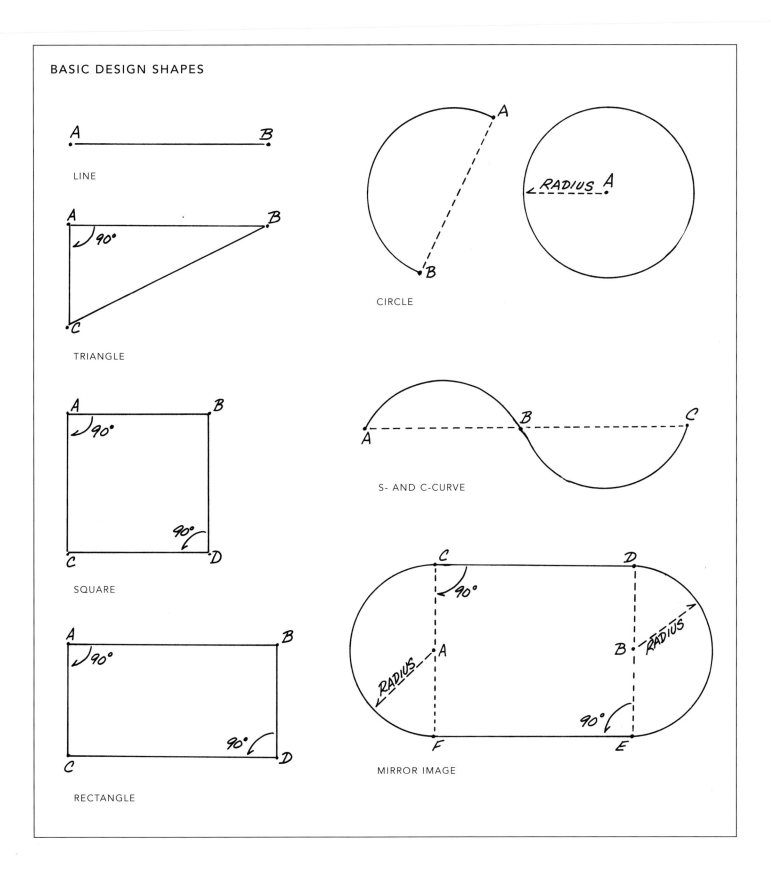

LINE

TRIANGLE

SQUARE

RECTANGLE

CIRCLE

S- AND C-CURVE

MIRROR IMAGE

LINE
(see p. 16)

Line designs, triangular patterns, and square or rectangular sketches accent the basic form of woodworking by following the line of the furniture's structural members. A straight line design used along the sides of a hutch door can create vertical lift, enhancing the height of the project. Used across the drawer fronts of a bureau, the line design will visually pull the eye along the full length of the drawer, making the bureau appear to be more expansive than it is.

The triangular design reinforces the joinery of the wood structure by placing emphasis on the intersections of the different elements that create the furniture. Triangular patterns visually strengthen the angles and corners. Whereas a line design will accent one plane, either vertical or horizontal, a triangular design can emphasize the corner points, bringing the eye to the perimeter of the structure's frame.

Square and rectangular designs draw the eye to individual areas of the wood structure. They focus the viewer on specific elements, such as door panels, box lids, and chest fronts, and reenforce the basic shape that is used in woodworking.

Circular and oval patterns give more emphasis to the design. These patterns directly oppose the structural shape of the project, creating a pleasing contradiction for the viewer. By pulling the eye away from the hard, static edges of the work, a curved pattern can soften the general appearance of the furniture.

TRIANGLE
(see p. 43)

**RECTANGLE**
*(see p. 59)*

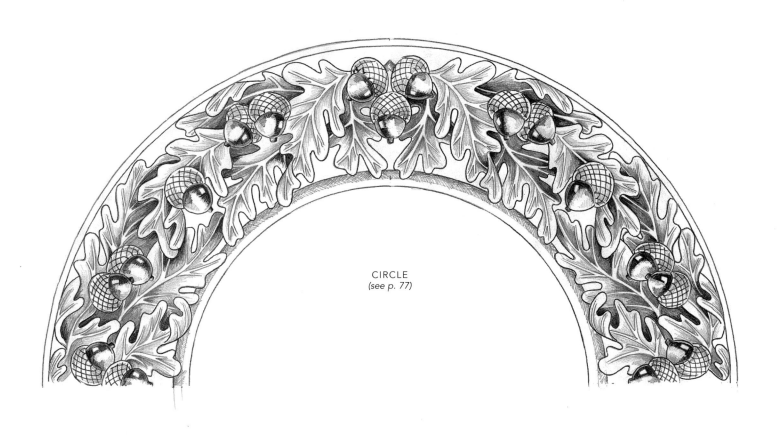

**CIRCLE**
*(see p. 77)*

S-CURVE
*(see p. 99)*

MIRROR IMAGE
*(see p. 113)*

The S-curve and the C-curve are very free-flowing patterns that complement nature. These patterns open up the structural form by accentuating both the height of the project with one part of the design and the width with other parts.

The mirror image is a design shape widely used in woodworking. This type of pattern allows you to use an open, flowing pattern within the confines of an angular structure. By focusing the eye on a central line down the wood form, you can reach in any direction and accent any area. Once the central line is established, you can embellish the structure of the furniture with curving headboards and aprons.

Free-form scenes are open-edged designs that are self-contained by their interrelated elements. Here the structural element of the wood on which they are used creates the final shape of the design. Often the free-form pattern is marked from one line within the design. An example would be a reference line drawn from wing tip to wing tip on an American eagle design. Although free-form patterns may occupy the entire area of the wood, using a general reference line will make the placement of the pattern easier.

Although the seven basic shapes may seem to cover a wide range of possible designs, there will always be one design that just does not seem to fit into any category. Remember that the basic shapes are used only for planning the final look of the design on the furniture and for easier placement on individual wood pieces. The basic shape will not be carved or burned—it is only for reference. Therefore, when a design does not fit into a general shape category, you can choose an arbitrary shape that overlays the design. This arbitrary shape now provides the reference points for measuring.

Some designs fit more than one category. In the chapters that follow, I've grouped the patterns by basic design shape, but there is a certain amount of overlap. Don't be surprised to find a mirror-image design in the chapter on line designs, or even a circular pattern in the chapter on squares and rectangles.

FREE-FORM
*(see p. 152)*

# 2

# LINE DESIGNS

From a simple beaded line to the complex interlacing of grapevines, line designs create visual movement across the face of the furniture. By accenting one direction, either vertical or horizontal, you can move the viewer from one structural element to another while emphasizing either the height of the work or the length.

Simple beaded lines, roundover edges, and ogees are basic woodworking enhancements. You can expand these straight line designs with a natural or geometric element. By adding a small overlay to the basic line, you can create areas of emphasis for the viewer. Corners, drawer handles, and central points are excellent areas to add a visual surprise.

Line designs are also made up of repeating units, which make it easy to create designs of a given length that will match the structural form. Repetitive units create a visual ruler for the viewer, a way to mark the size of the form. When using repetitive units the final look of the line design can be changed by reversing the units at the central point, by reversing the pattern every unit, or by mixing different sizes of units throughout the line.

Mirror-image line designs keep the free-flowing shape of natural elements while pulling the eye away from a central point on the structure. This type of design may be changed throughout the work by inverting the mirror image from one structural area to another.

BEADED LINE

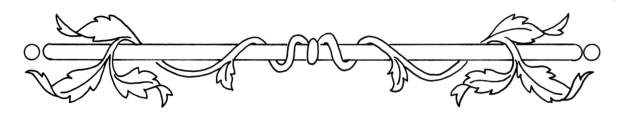

REPETITIVE LINE

MIRROR IMAGE

Line-design patterns need not be composed of straight lines only. Using a flowing or curving line can soften the final effect of the furniture and still give vertical or horizontal emphasis. Adding a gentle curve or loop to the main line of the pattern breaks any long expanses across the structure (see the drawings below).

To place a line design on the wood for carving, burning, or painting, you need to establish a reference line through the pattern and determine the length of the line design. The reference line can be used to ensure that the pattern is parallel to the edge of the wood element. To center the design, first subtract the length of the pattern from the length of the wood

element. Then divide this measurement in half to find the distance the design needs to be placed from either side of the wood element (see the top drawing on the facing page).

Line designs work well on table aprons and trestles, hutch valances and toeboards, molding-strip areas, drawer fronts, and the stiles or rails along door fronts. When using a line design, choose one main direction for the pattern. This keeps the viewer's eye moving easily up and down or back and forth across the form. If the pattern changes direction, it can be visually confusing and make the finished piece seem disconnected.

Line designs created with gently curving elements can be confined within parallel reference lines for placement.

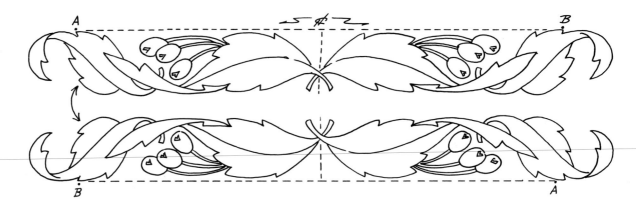

The addition of holly leaves and berries softens what would otherwise be a static, crisp line across the surface of the wood.

## LINE-DESIGN PLACEMENT

To place a line design with accuracy, mark a straight line through the pattern and register it to a corresponding line on the wood structure.

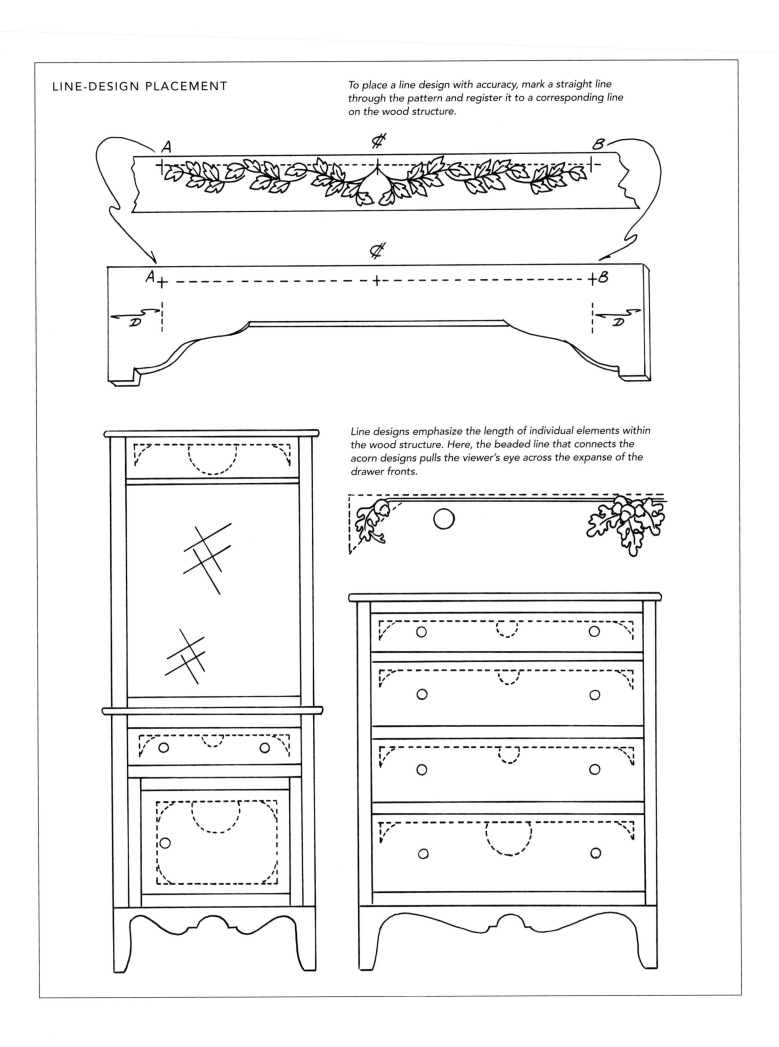

Line designs emphasize the length of individual elements within the wood structure. Here, the beaded line that connects the acorn designs pulls the viewer's eye across the expanse of the drawer fronts.

HOLLY SWAG

OCTOBER BERRIES

OAK AND ACORNS

STYLIZED THISTLE

SINGLE-LEAF END

TWISTED-LEAF OVERLAY

SCROLL END

TRIPLE-LEAF END

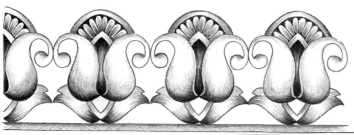

STYLIZED TULIPS

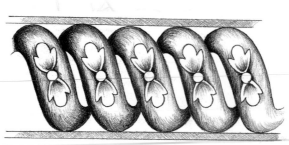

PATTERNED TWIST

TEARDROPS

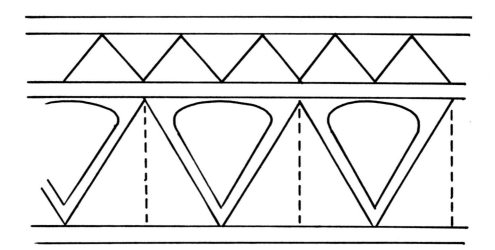

ARROWHEADS

WROUGHT-IRON TWIST

SPLIT STYLIZED TULIP

IRON HEART

HALF-DAISY TURN

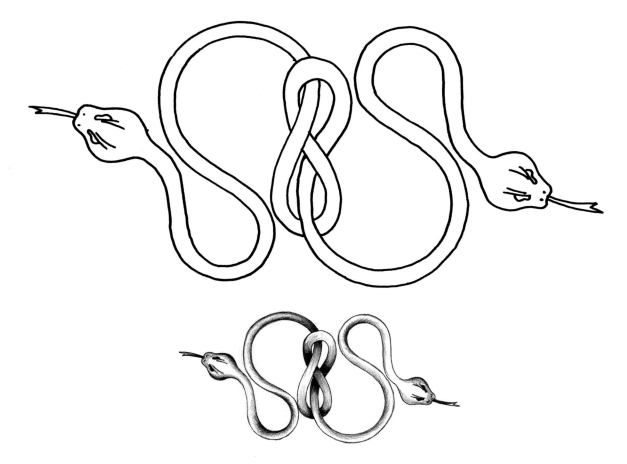

KNOTTED SNAKE

IRON-LEAF CIRCLES

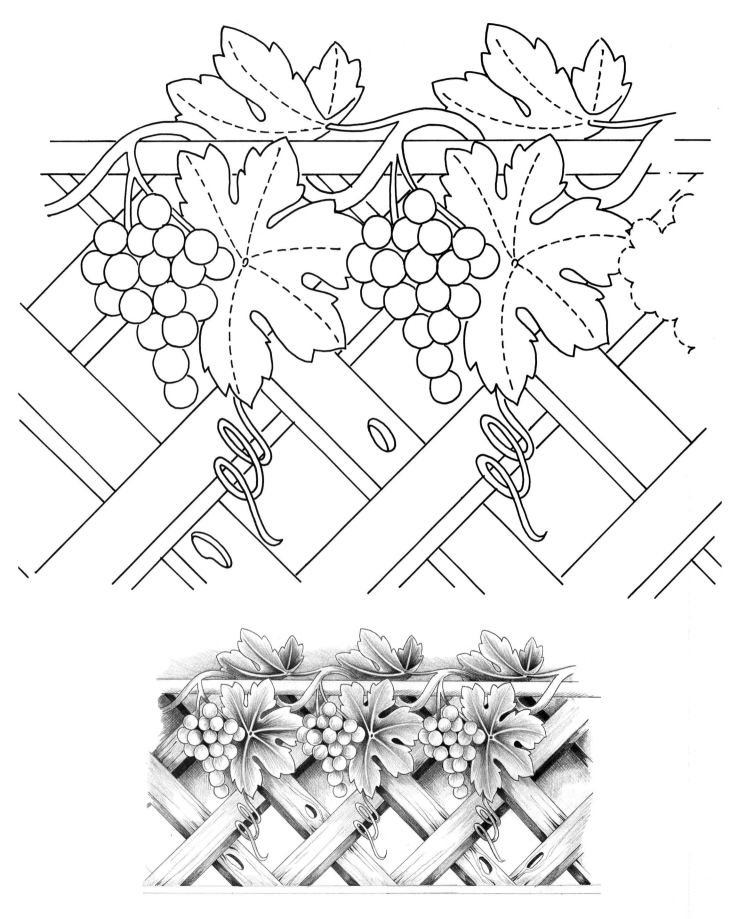

HARVEST LATTICE

POD AND PETAL LATTICE

POD AND PETAL LEAF

RIBBON AND BEADED LINE

# 3

# TRIANGULAR DESIGNS

Whereas line designs emphasize the vertical or horizontal structure of the wood form and square designs bring the focus to the repetitive rectangles of the furniture, triangular designs draw the viewer's eye to the corners of the work. By using this pattern style, the vertical supports of the woodwork are united with the horizontal structures.

The corners and right angles of a piece of furniture are areas of joinery, either where two pieces of wood come together or where two separate units of the furniture form are in contact. These areas are ideal for pattern work. A triangular design visually pushes against the corner in which it is placed. This thrust can be used to accent the final size of the piece by focusing on the four corners of the form. Height can be accentuated by using triangular patterns along only the top edge of an element.

In woodcarving, the triangular pattern can be extended into lattice and pierce-work additions to the final furniture form. Along the upper corners of an open-front hutch, carvings that fit into the right angles not only enhance the shelf area with design but also seem to support the hutch top.

Not all triangular patterns must have three straight sides. A pattern that is created with one right angle can have an inner side that curves, thereby breaking the crisp, angular feel of the design. This feature makes the triangular pattern an excellent frame for circular or oval designs (see the drawing at right). A circle pattern might be used on the door panels with a triangular pattern that has a curved side in the corners of the door frame (see the drawing on p. 30).

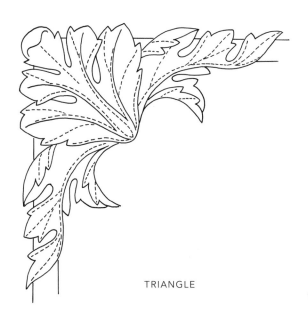

TRIANGLE

TRIANGLE AS FRAME

To transfer a triangular pattern to the wood, use the lines of the right angle and a measured point along each side as reference marks. These marks can easily be measured from the right angle on the wood elements. Once the pattern is marked, it can be inverted from top to bottom on the furniture or reversed from side to side (see the drawing on the facing page).

Since most triangular designs are used in the corners or right angle of the wood form, a word about joinery is appropriate. When choosing the furniture piece or area to enhance, consider the joinery used in the wood structure before you begin your pattern work. Dovetails, finger joints, inlaid joints, and some forms of Japanese joinery are decorative in themselves. Pattern work should complement the final form not compete with it. Placing a pattern or design over a highly detailed piece of joinery de-emphasizes both the pattern and the joinery and creates a visually confusing area to the viewer. Remember that fine joinery work is in itself an art and does not need an accent.

Equally important, do not use a pattern to try to conceal poorly constructed joinery. If there is a problem with the original joint work, the problem will still be there underneath the pattern and design work. In this case, the viewer's eye is drawn to the very area that you wish to minimize. It is better to recut the original joinery than to try and hide it.

## CREATING A "FRAME" WITH TRIANGULAR DESIGNS

*The triangular patterns used in the corners frame the central circular designs and unite them with the rectangular shape of the door panels.*

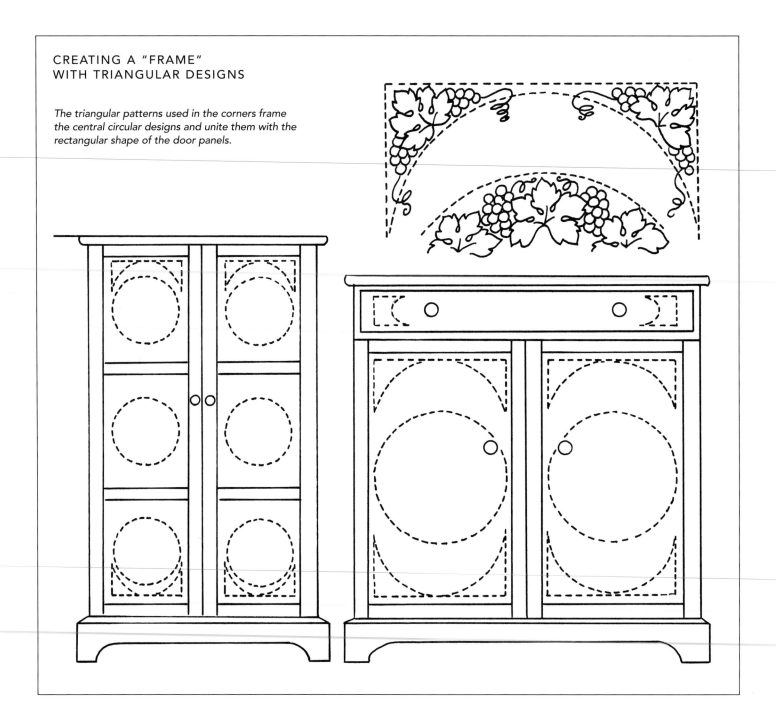

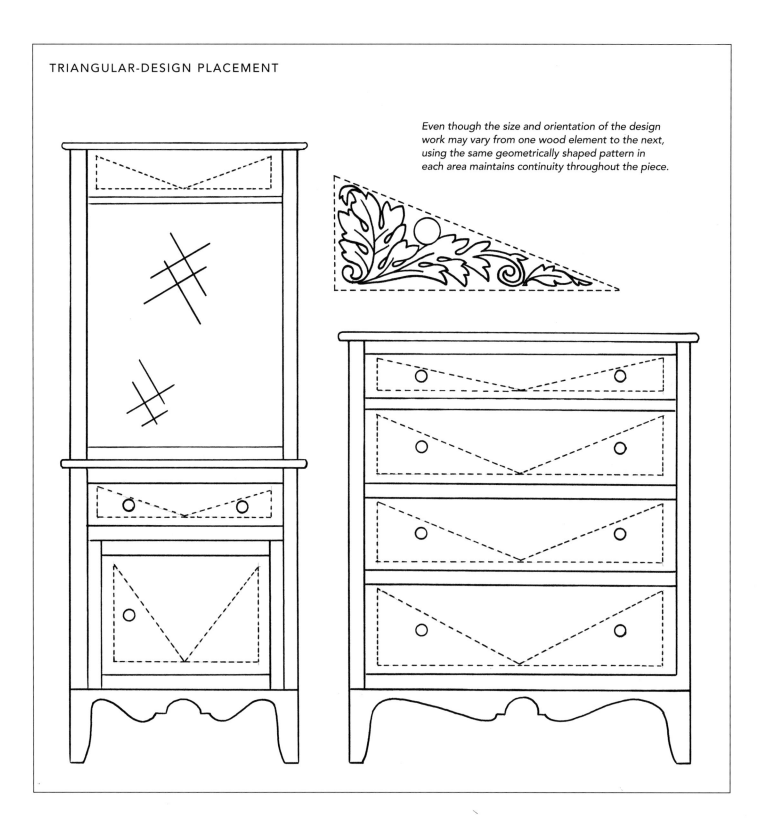

# TRIANGULAR-DESIGN PLACEMENT

*Even though the size and orientation of the design work may vary from one wood element to the next, using the same geometrically shaped pattern in each area maintains continuity throughout the piece.*

POINSETTIA ROSETTE

MARASCHINO CHERRIES

FLUTED SHELL

VICTORIAN LEAVES

ROSE-LEAF CURL

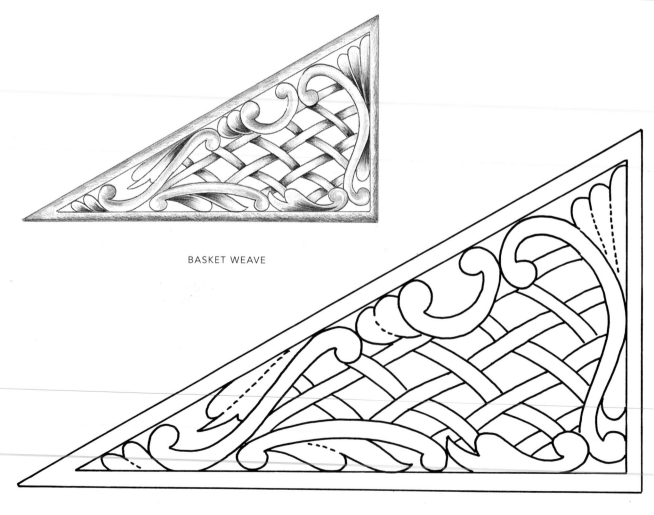

BASKET WEAVE

REMBRANDT TULIPS

CATHEDRAL CORNER

ARCHED ACANTHUS

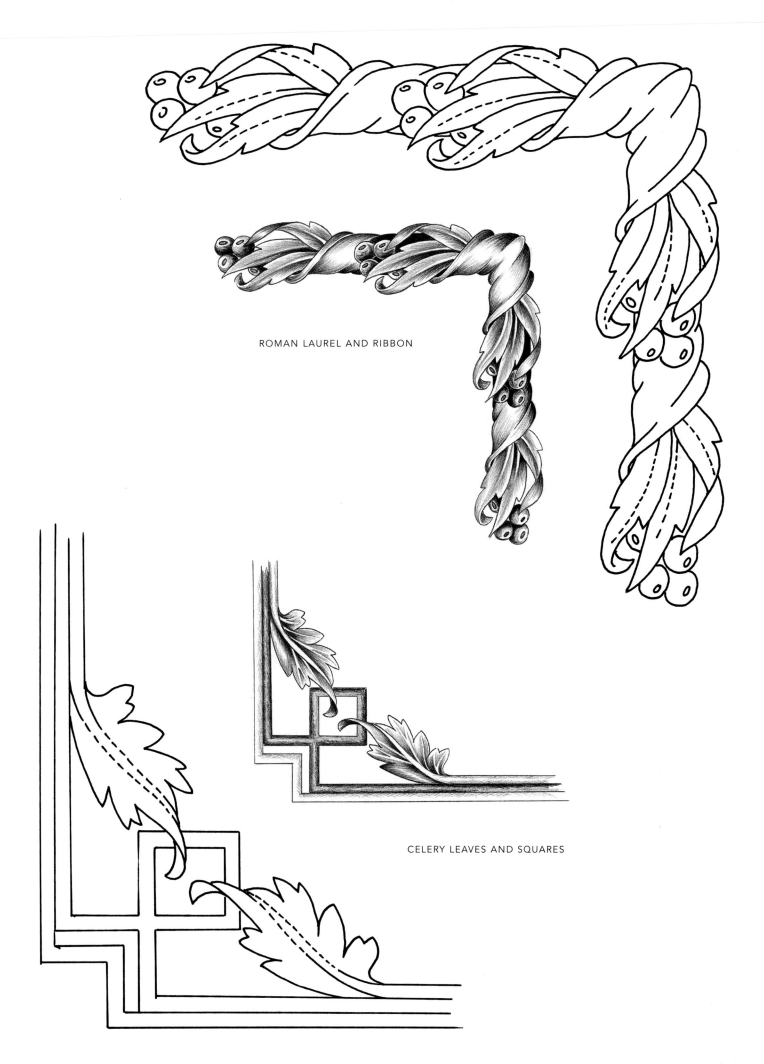

ROMAN LAUREL AND RIBBON

CELERY LEAVES AND SQUARES

TWIST AND TURNS

SUMMER ROSES
(outer corner)

HERALDRY LEAVES

SIMPLE ROSE

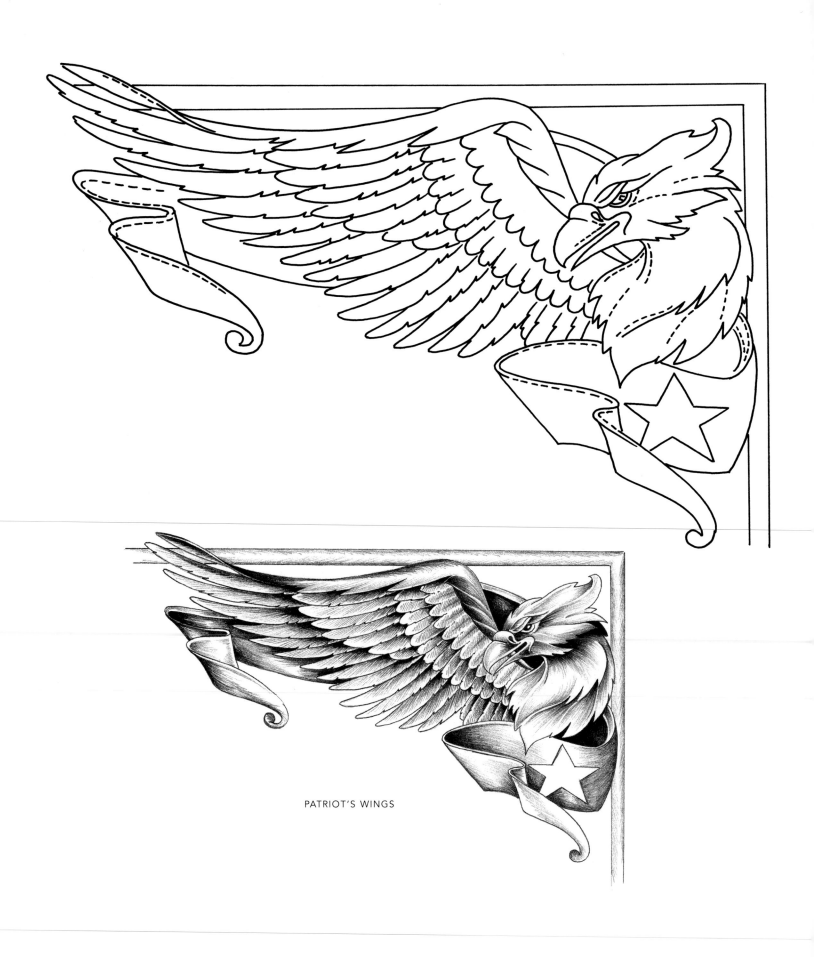

PATRIOT'S WINGS

LEATHER AND LATTICE

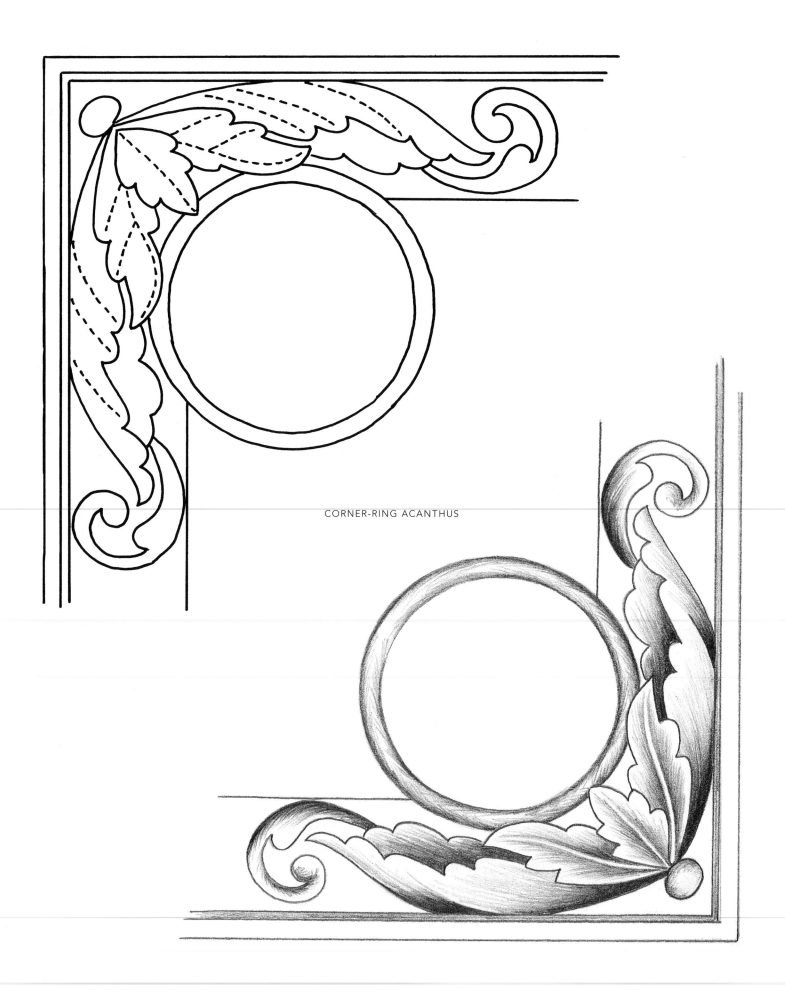

CORNER-RING ACANTHUS

SUMMER ROSES
(inner corner)

# 4

# SQUARE & RECTANGULAR DESIGNS

Line designs readily change into square or rectangular designs simply by turning the corner. These designs allow you to take the pattern along the perimeter of the structure and emphasize the box forms of the furniture (see the drawing at right). By using an even margin along each side of the square or rectangular design, the size of the element on which the pattern is used is visually strengthened.

Turning the corner with a line design can be accomplished in several ways. First, you can allow one element of the line design to touch the same element at the 45° line in the corner (Drawing 1 at right). Since this configuration will reverse the pattern at the corners, you'll need to compensate by finding the center point of each side segment and flipping the pattern over to direct it toward the next corner.

A second way to turn the corner is to continue the pattern in one direction through the corner intersections (Drawing 2 at right). In this design, one element at the beginning of the pattern always touches one element at the end of the pattern, and every pattern segment is laid down in the same direction.

Using a square or rectangular design emphasizes the structural lines of the furniture.

1          2          3

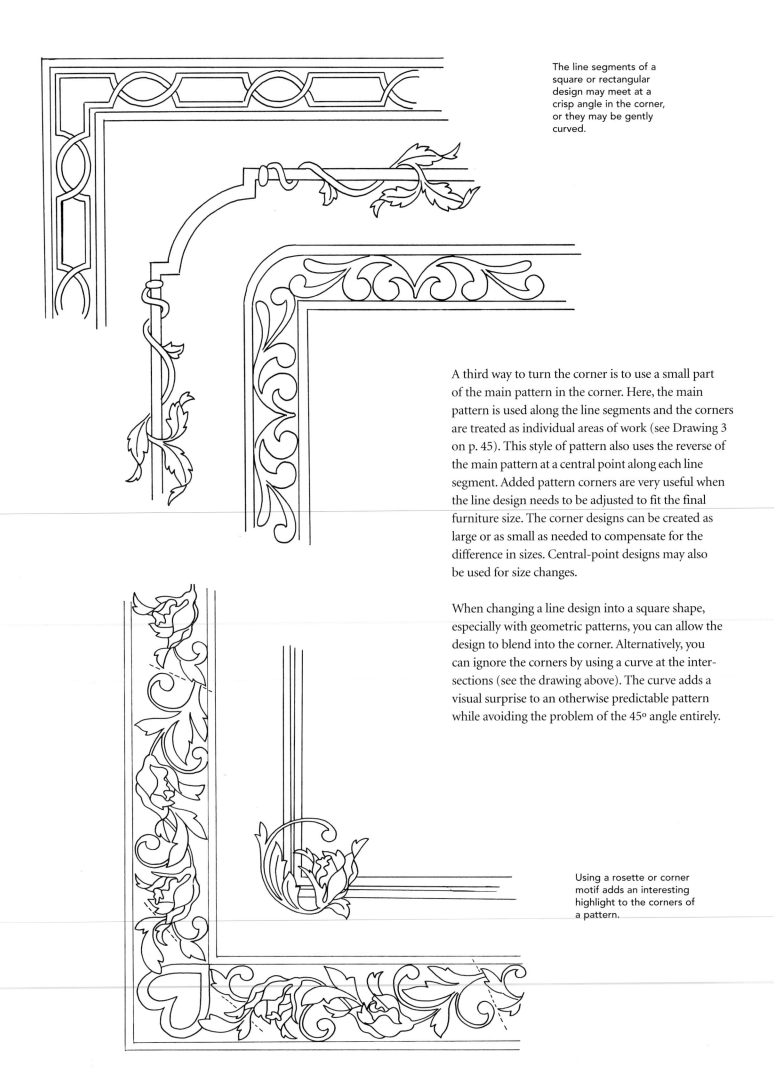

The line segments of a
square or rectangular
design may meet at a
crisp angle in the corner,
or they may be gently
curved.

A third way to turn the corner is to use a small part
of the main pattern in the corner. Here, the main
pattern is used along the line segments and the corners
are treated as individual areas of work (see Drawing 3
on p. 45). This style of pattern also uses the reverse of
the main pattern at a central point along each line
segment. Added pattern corners are very useful when
the line design needs to be adjusted to fit the final
furniture size. The corner designs can be created as
large or as small as needed to compensate for the
difference in sizes. Central-point designs may also
be used for size changes.

When changing a line design into a square shape,
especially with geometric patterns, you can allow the
design to blend into the corner. Alternatively, you
can ignore the corners by using a curve at the intersections (see the drawing above). The curve adds a
visual surprise to an otherwise predictable pattern
while avoiding the problem of the 45° angle entirely.

Using a rosette or corner
motif adds an interesting
highlight to the corners of
a pattern.

Rosette designs can be created to fill the corner areas of a square design. Just as in a door frame, the rosette in design work joins a vertical design to a horizontal design with a corner pattern or motif. This pattern may be part of the line design used in the general pattern work—as in the frame of the lion drawing below where the corner motif repeats the curve of the geometric units—or it may be something completely different. An example of the latter would be a beaded line that uses a rosebud pattern to highlight the corner, or a line design of wild roses with a heart design in the corner (see the bottom drawing on the facing page).

Square and rectangular designs are sometimes used to contain free-form patterns, just as a picture frame contains or surrounds a painting. In this type of format the design reaches out to the edges of the square but does not go beyond its lines; for example, the lion pattern below is captured within the boundaries of the geometric design.

A square or rectangular design can be used to frame a free-form pattern.

Triangular patterns can be combined to create a
square shape. Repeating a triangle in each of the four
corners and allowing the patterns to connect along
the sides gives the final appearance of a square or rectangle (see the drawing at right). Also, working with
the triangular pattern laid along the diagonal axes of
the square can create a balanced, four-sided shape
(see the drawing above). For some ideas on how to use
these designs on furniture, see the drawing on p. 50.

Square and rectangular designs are extremely complementary to woodworking because they reflect the basic shape of furniture elements (see the drawing below). They may be used to accent door panels, chest lids, and drawers. When determining the placement of a square or rectangular design, you must consider the difference in size between the edge of the wood and the edge of the pattern. The margins can be equal on all four sides, which will place the design centrally in the wood element, or they can be wider at the side or top and bottom edges. Making the side margins wider emphasizes the height of the wood element, whereas using wider margins along the top and bottom of the design accents the width of the furniture form.

Use the outer perimeter of the rectangle and its four corner points as reference marks when transferring the pattern. By marking the desired margins and the four corner points onto the wood element, you now have marks that correspond to the pattern.

## RECTANGULAR-DESIGN PLACEMENT

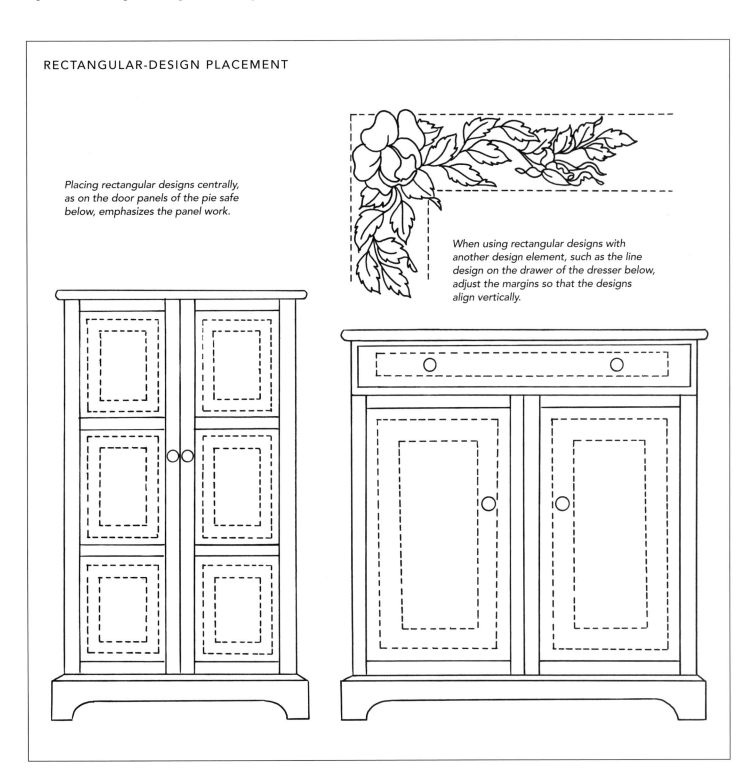

*Placing rectangular designs centrally, as on the door panels of the pie safe below, emphasizes the panel work.*

*When using rectangular designs with another design element, such as the line design on the drawer of the dresser below, adjust the margins so that the designs align vertically.*

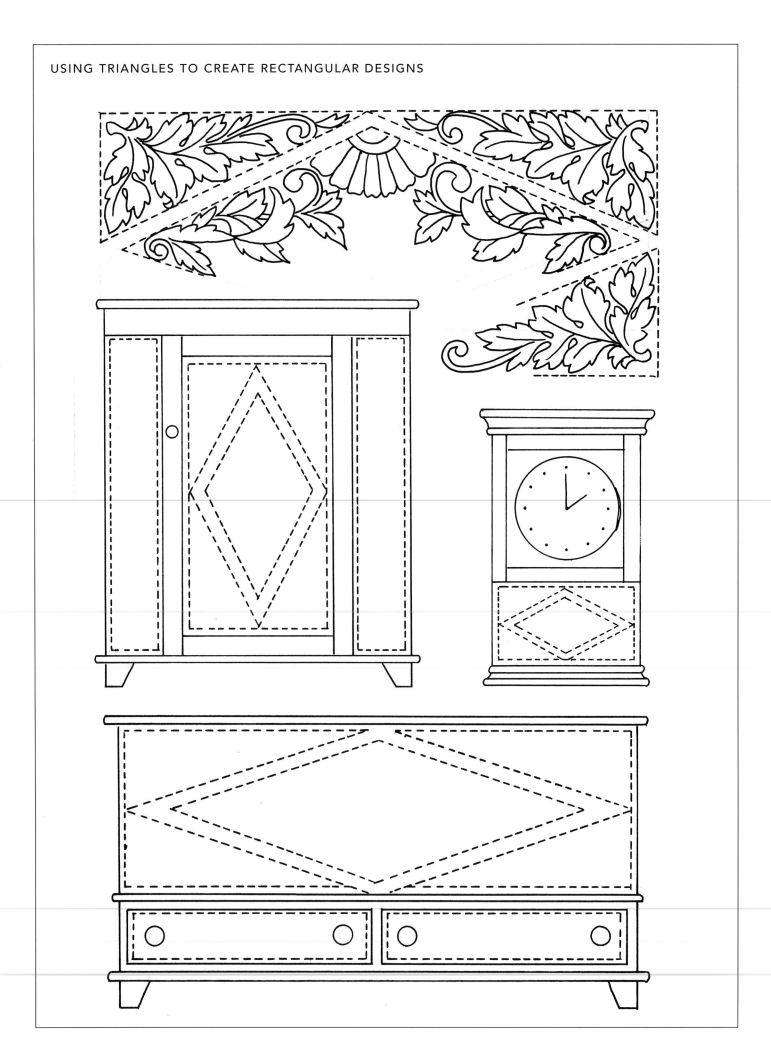

TRUMPET-VINE CLOCK

ROLLED SHELL

REMBRANDT-TULIPS PANEL

LACE-LEAF CLOCK FACE

CARNATION-PILLOW PANEL

CELTIC-BRAID PANEL

SMALL FLORAL CLOCK

DIAMOND LEAVES

# 5

# CIRCULAR & OVAL DESIGNS

When you use a circular or an oval design, the emphasis is pulled away from the angular lines of the furniture and brought to the soft curves that contain the design. This pattern style places more importance on the carving (or wood burning or painting) since it is created with boundaries that are not directly related to those of the structure on which it is placed. This gentle conflict between, say, the rectangle of a door panel and the oval of a leaf pattern that has been over-laid upon it is a dynamic combination.

The circular design automatically creates its own margins on the wood element, leaving the corners free of design. Because of the basic shape of the pattern work and the corner transition area between the pattern and the perimeter of the wood element, using a circular design can minimize the chance of over-powering the furniture with design work.

The circle around each of these farm scenes both frames the barn landscape and accents the curve of the leaf ribbon.

Leaving a circular design open along one edge helps it blend into the wood on which it is placed.

Whether to use a circle or an oval to contain the design is determined by the shape of the wood element on which it is to be placed. A well-balanced pattern will have equal margins in the corners of the structure. Therefore, rectangular doors visually require oval designs, while square panels call for circular patterns.

The artwork doesn't need to be contained completely within a circle. Using a half-circle along the top of the pattern and allowing the curved lines to blend into a rectangular shape at the bottom can give the work a very uplifting look. This technique works especially well to accent tall door panels or to break up long horizontal elements, as on a blanket-chest front (see the drawing below). Leaving part of the circle open to the wood element on which it is placed can blend the design into the wood (see the drawing at left).

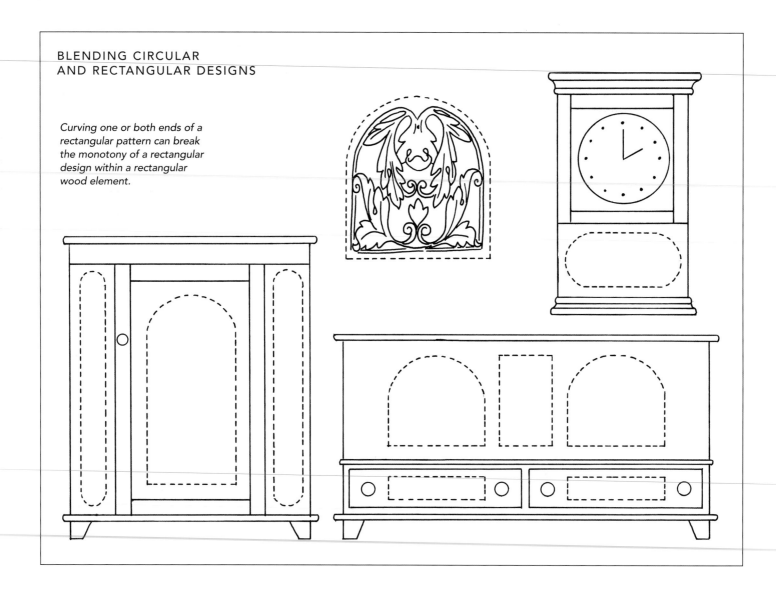

### BLENDING CIRCULAR AND RECTANGULAR DESIGNS

*Curving one or both ends of a rectangular pattern can break the monotony of a rectangular design within a rectangular wood element.*

By adding a curve to both ends of a rectangle, you can create an elongated oval design, as shown in the drawing above. Another way to use a circular pattern to modify a rectangular design is to add a curved line to the center of the rectangle, which serves to break up the angular feel of the structure (see the drawing on p. 64).

The corners that are created by using a circular design within a square wood element can be areas for additional design work. Left bare, the unworked space emphasizes the curve of the pattern within an angular wood element. Carved with a triangular pattern that contains a curved side toward the circle, the corners can accent the conflict between the two shapes. Here, a pattern that's complementary to the circular design can reinforce the transition from the softness of the curve to the crispness of the angular lines (see the drawing at right).

To place a circular design on the wood, begin by drawing diagonals between opposite corners to find the central point of the wood element. Using a compass, you can now establish the diameter of the circle to be used. Allow a margin around the pattern so that it doesn't extend completely to the edge of the wood. If the pattern work will include curved triangles in the corner, mark two circles from the central point, one for the main pattern and the other to define the curved inside edge of the triangular pattern. To ensure accuracy, whenever possible use a compass to trace the circles directly to the work.

On arched patterns that are made with a half-circle top that blends into a rectangle at the bottom, use the two right angles at the bottom of the design for placement. Allow an equal margin along all the sides and from the upper point of the circle.

Oval patterns may be placed by matching the centerlines of the pattern and the wood element. Again, allow equal margins at the upper and lower points of the oval for even spacing.

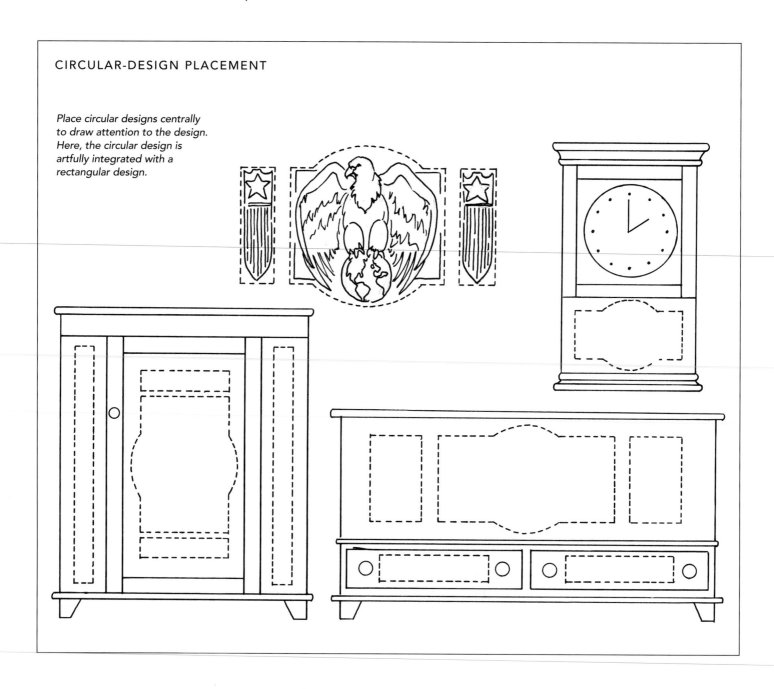

## CIRCULAR-DESIGN PLACEMENT

*Place circular designs centrally to draw attention to the design. Here, the circular design is artfully integrated with a rectangular design.*

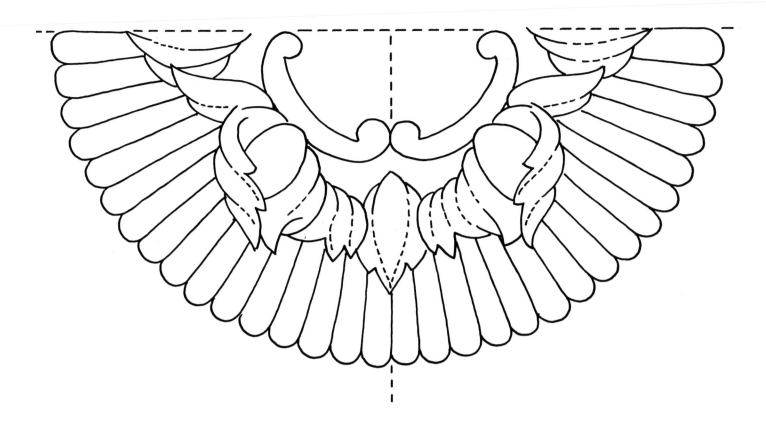

SHELL CIRCLE

HAY-BARN CIRCLE

MILKING-BARN CIRCLE

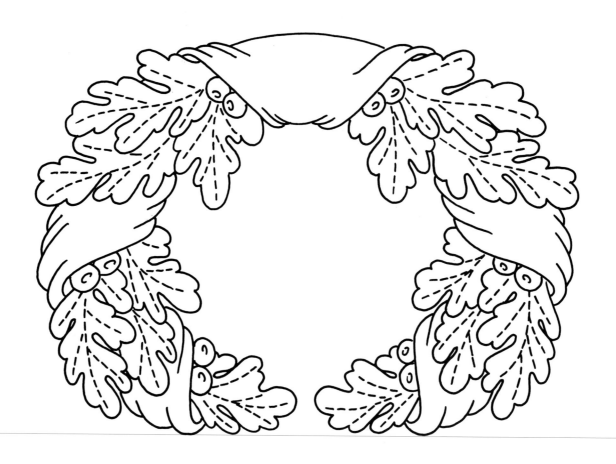

SMALL VICTORY WREATH

SWEETHEART OVAL

WROUGHT-IRON FEATHERS

VINE AND BERRIES OVAL

BOW AND BERRIES RING

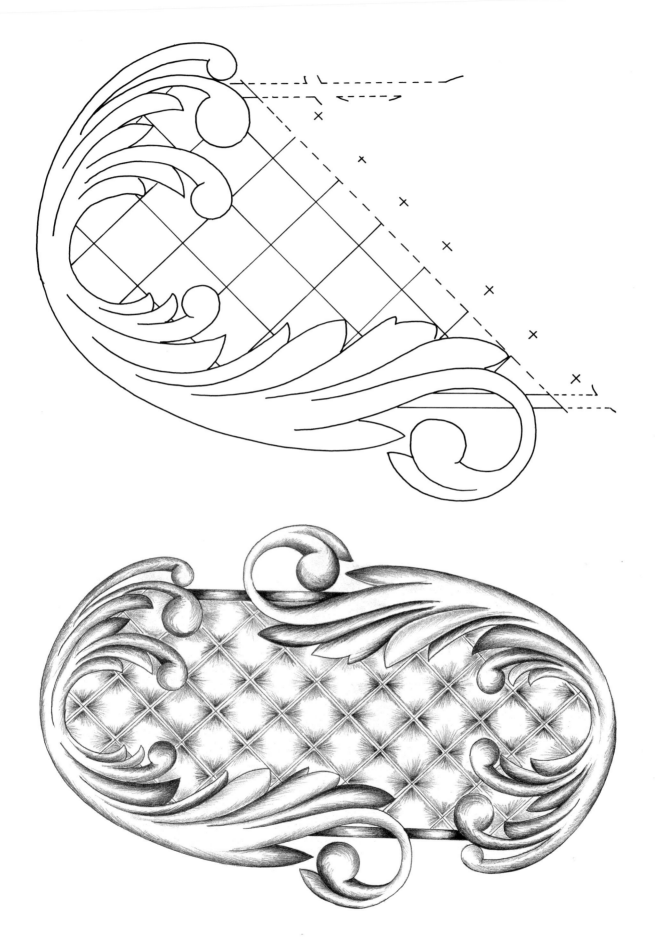

SCROLL-PILLOW PANEL

SIMPLE SCROLL

CURLED SWAG

WILD-ROSE CIRCLE

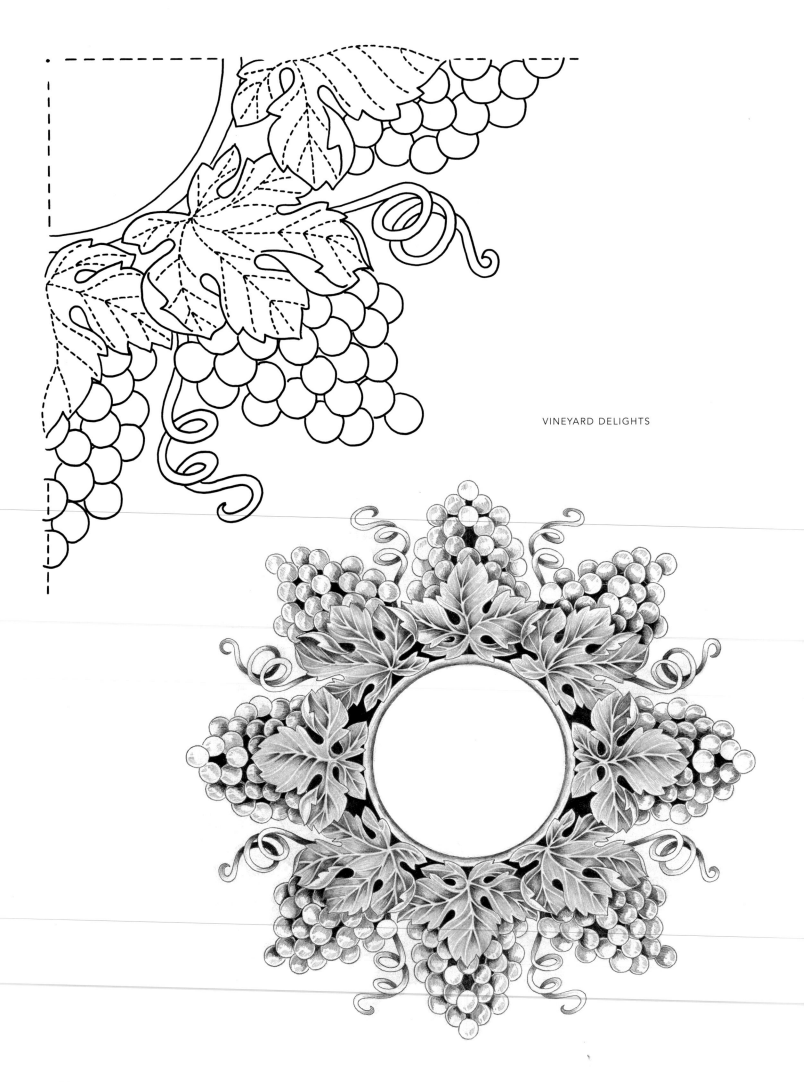

VINEYARD DELIGHTS

HARVEST CIRCLE

ROSE-ACCENTED FAN

TULIP OVAL

## ✿ 6 ✿
# S- & C-CURVE DESIGNS

Of all the design shapes that can be used in wood-working, the S-curve and the C-curve are the most complementary to nature. With these designs, the pattern flows from one area of the wood element to another without a formal line to control it. This sense of flow makes S-curve and C-curve patterns ideal for designs that are created with leaves, flowers, berries, and branches. S- and C-curves allow you to accent whichever part of the piece you wish. Whereas circular designs soften the look of the furniture, curved patterns free it from its harsh angular look as they seem to float across the surface (see the drawing below).

### S- AND C-CURVE PLACEMENT

*Using a central curved pattern can soften the impact of the repetitive angular lines inherent in furniture construction.*

Most curved designs are worked as mirror images from the central line of the furniture. For example, if an S-curve is placed on one half of a drawer front, it would be reversed on the other half to maintain a balanced look (see the drawing above). Curved patterns may also be used on door panels to create a reflection of each other. Here, a C-curve or an S-curve may be placed facing the central rail between the doors, and the reverse of this curve may be placed on the opposite door to create a heart shape between the doors (see the drawing at left).

Scroll and ribbon designs also fall into the curved pattern category. Here, the flow of the line is determined by the flow of the scroll across the structure. This style of pattern is ideal when you want to include

Curved designs can be worked as mirror images from the central line of the furniture (top), or they can be used on adjoining panels to create a heart-shaped pattern (above).

Scroll and ribbon designs can be personalized to commemorate anniversaries and other events.

Simple curves create a flowing movement through the design.

writing within the design. Names, dates, or records of personal events become part of the design instead of an addendum to the pattern work. Including such personalizations in the design emphasizes their importance since the design is obviously created to commemorate this information (see the bottom drawing on the facing page).

To maintain the gentle flow of the pattern, try to keep the curves simple, as shown in the drawing above. Too many curves can be confusing to the viewer. Your goal is to create the soft feel of a gentle ocean wave, not the wild ride of a roller coaster.

When placing curved patterns on the wood structure, handle them as if they were straight-line designs. Find a straight line directly though the center of the pattern that allows an equal amount of design to either side of the line for balance (see the drawing at right). On this line establish two points, one toward each end of the pattern. The line and the two points may now be transferred to the wood structure, allowing easy placement of the pattern.

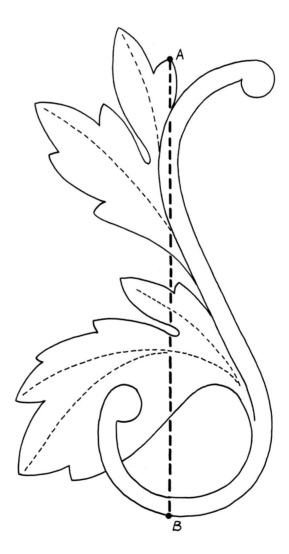

Curved designs may be placed on the wood from a vertical line centered through the pattern.

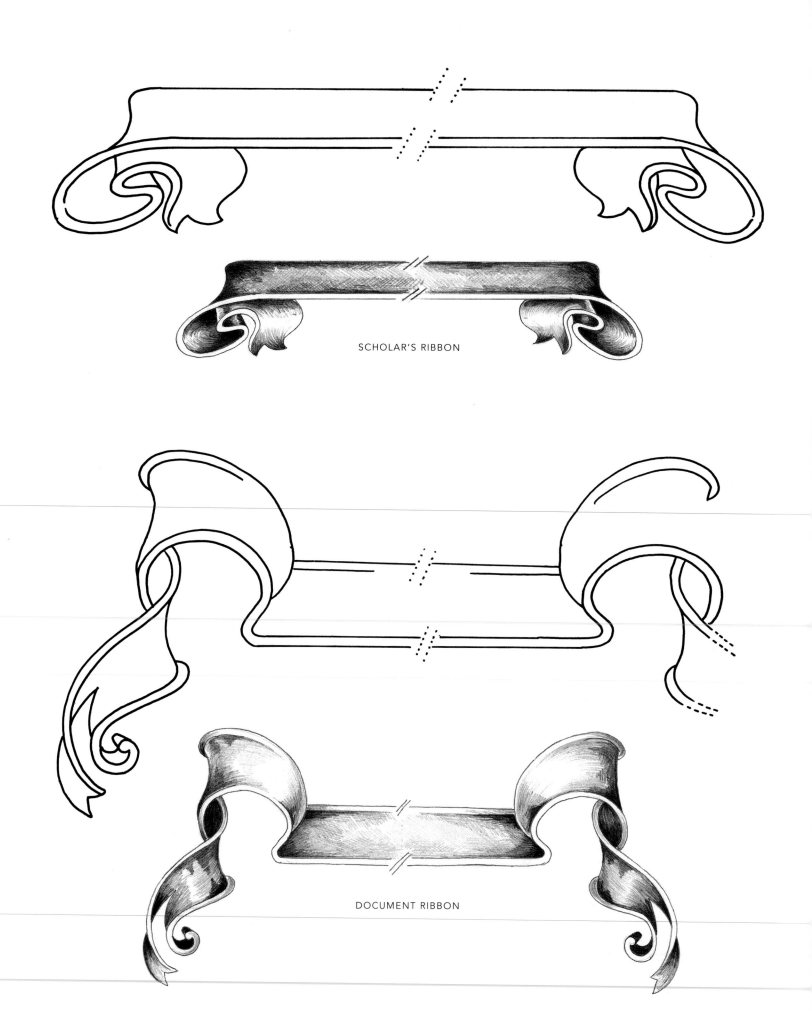

SCHOLAR'S RIBBON

DOCUMENT RIBBON

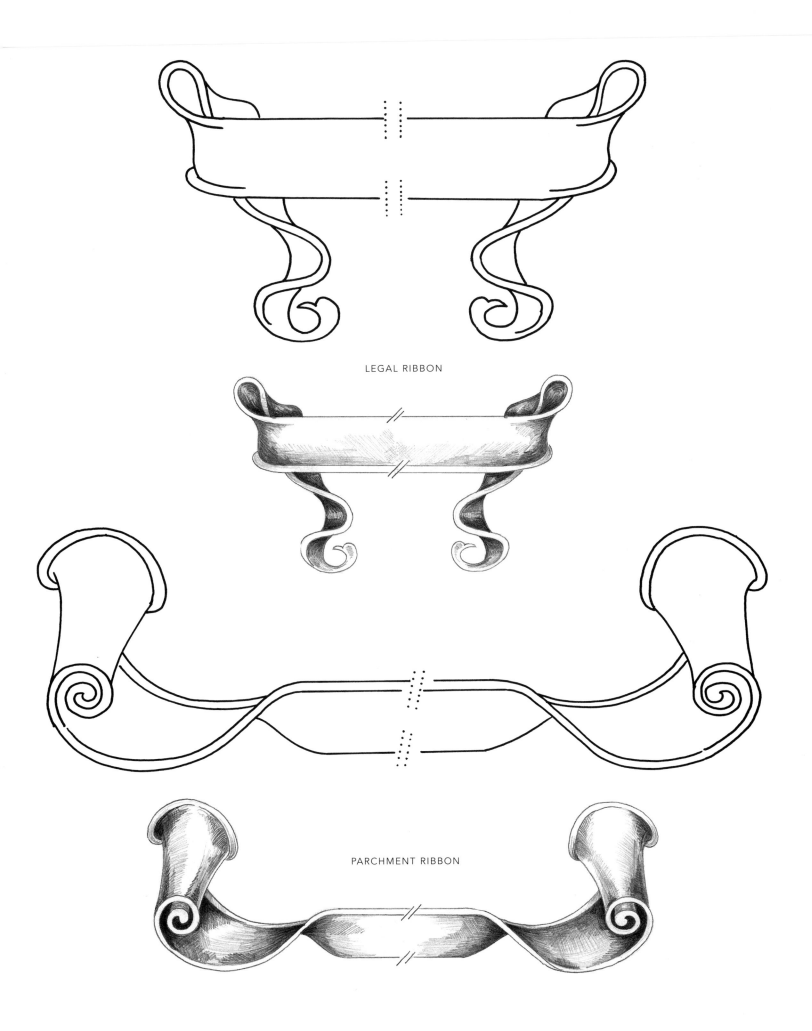

LEGAL RIBBON

PARCHMENT RIBBON

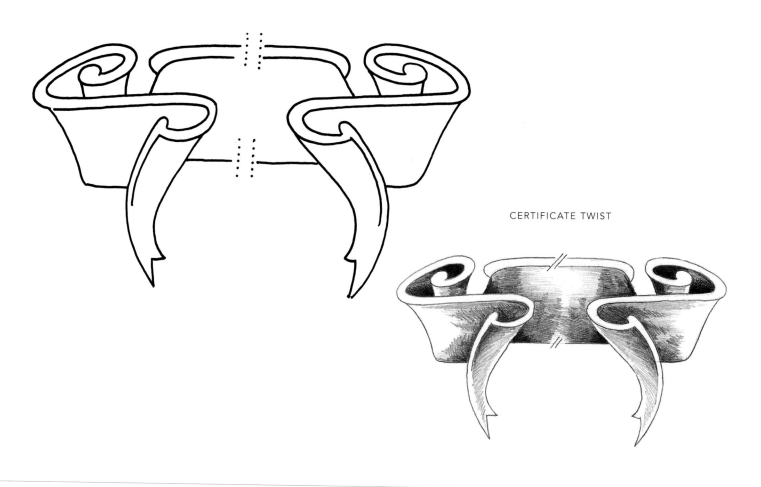

CERTIFICATE TWIST

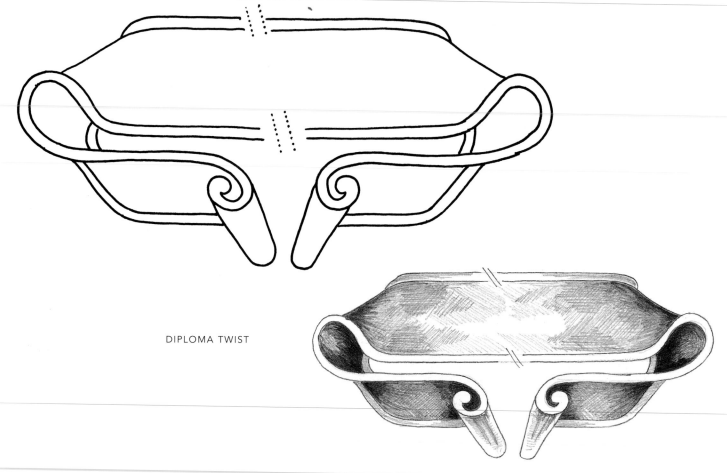

DIPLOMA TWIST

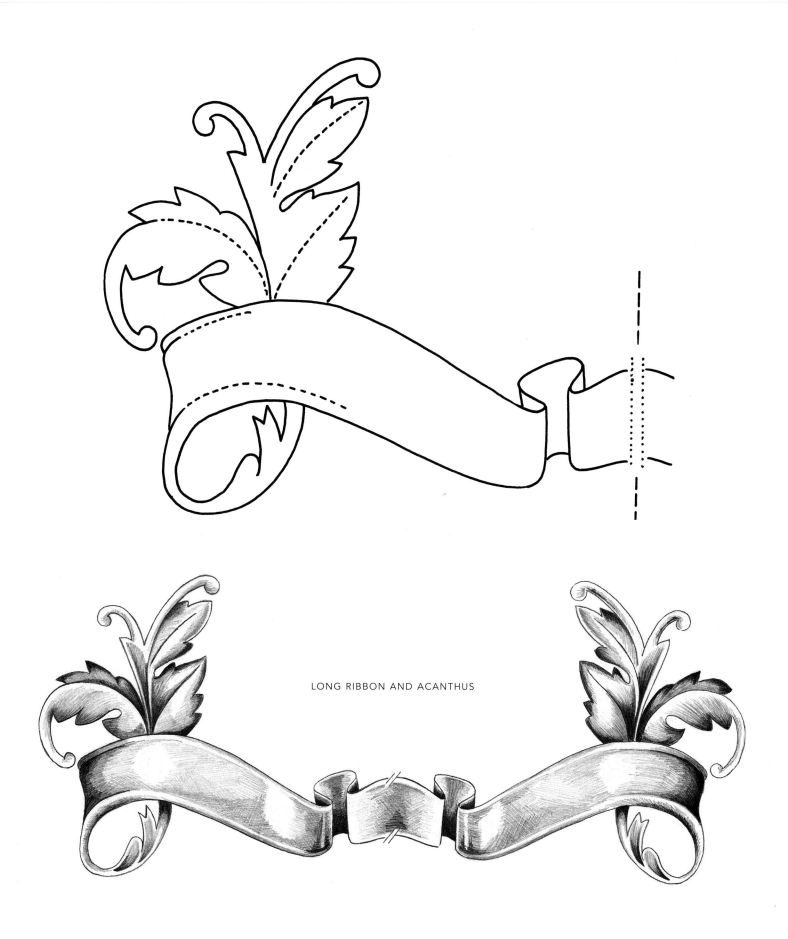

LONG RIBBON AND ACANTHUS

POMEGRANATE

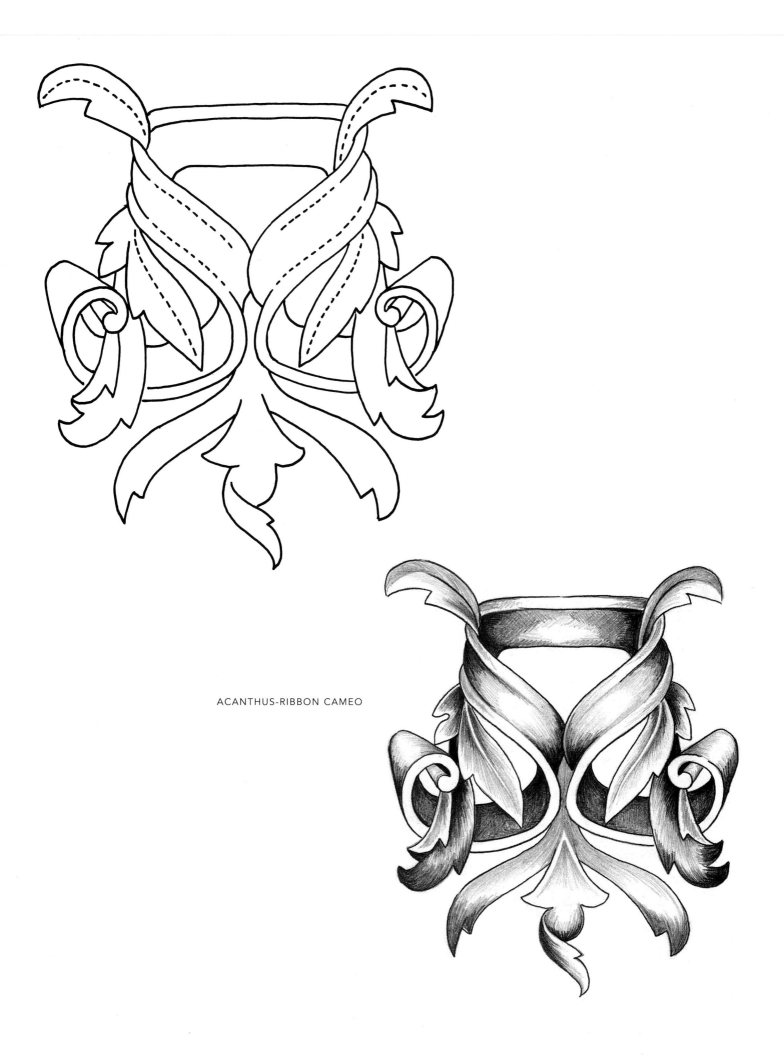

ACANTHUS-RIBBON CAMEO

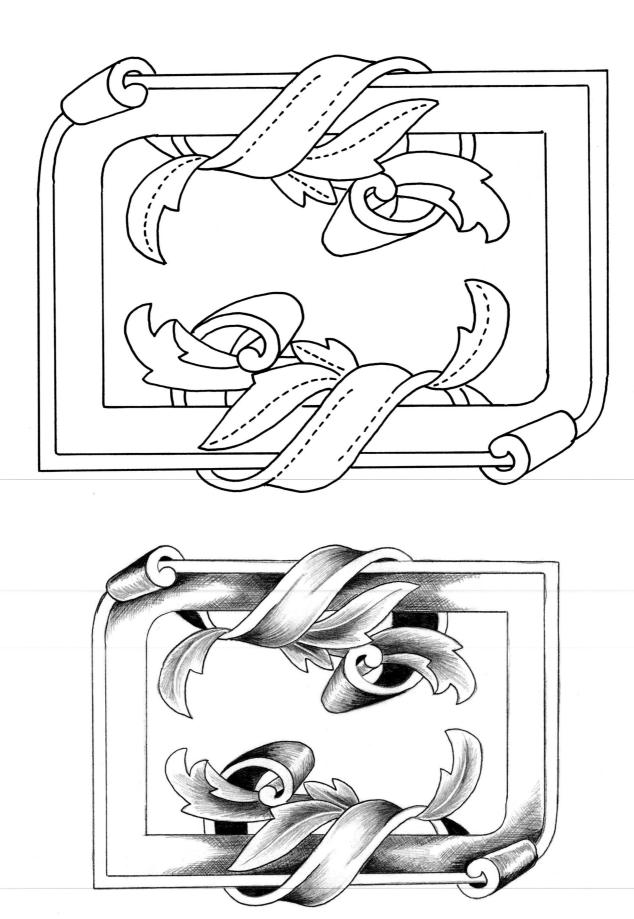

ACANTHUS-RIBBON FRAME

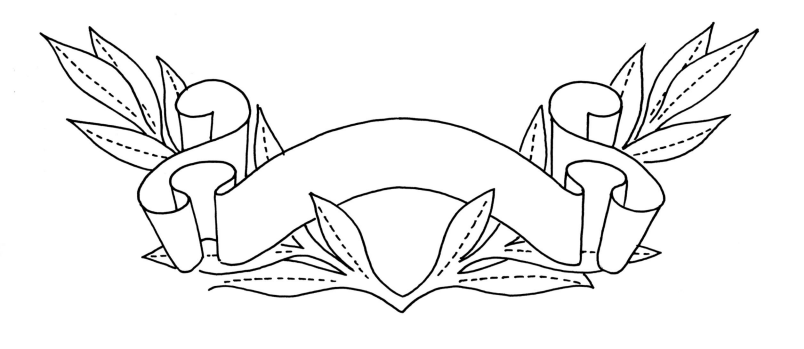

OLIVE-BRANCH SCROLL

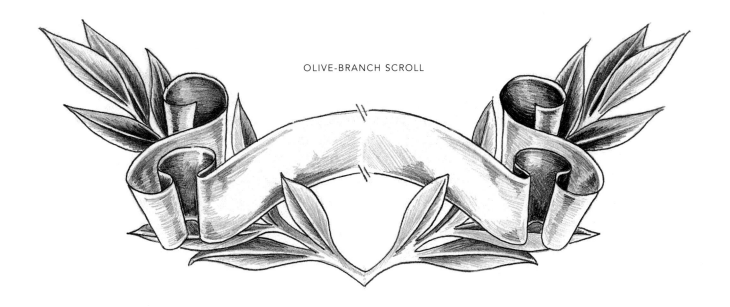

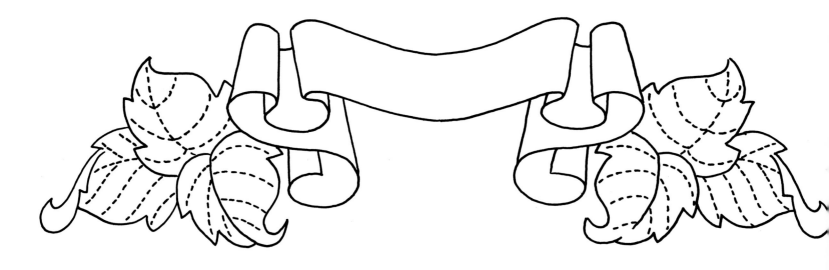

MULBERRY-LEAF SCROLL

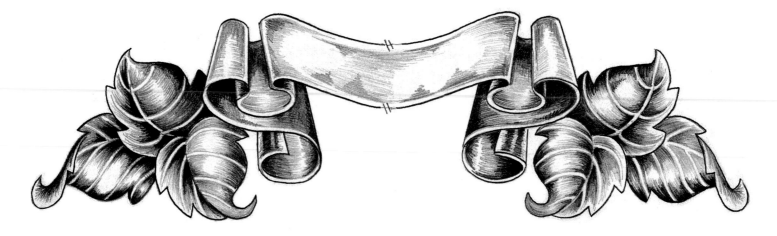

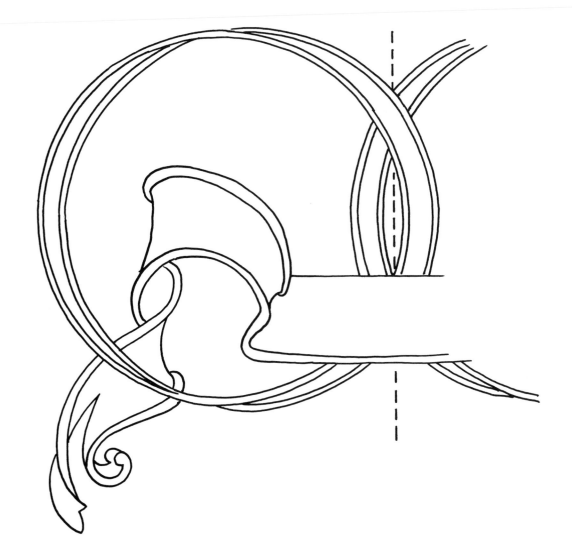

WEDDING-BANDS SCROLL

SEPARATED-PETALS SHELL

NINE-POINT SHELL

WINTER WHEAT

POMEGRANATE AND LEAVES

LARGE S-CURVE LEAF

LEAF AND SEED SHELL

SINGLE-SHELL LINE

LONG-SHELL CENTERPIECE

TRIPLE-SHELL LINE

LEAF BUNDLE

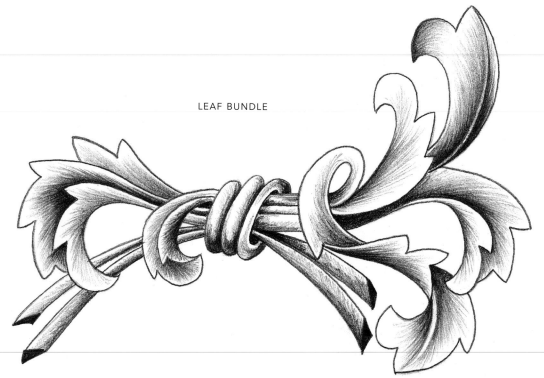

BACK-TURNED LEAVES

90°

CENTER LINE

LARGE HEART
TEMPLATE

# MIRROR-IMAGE DESIGNS

Of all the designs used in woodworking the mirror image lends itself most readily to large, creative expanses of artwork. Working from a central line, either vertical or horizontal, the pattern reaches outward across the face of the structure, repeating itself in reverse on the opposite side of the form. As with line designs and square designs, mirror images complement the basic structure of wood furniture.

A mirror-image design is created exactly as the name implies. One half of the pattern is drawn and then held against a mirror to see how it looks with its reflection. Using the mirror makes it possible to view the design work in progress and more easily direct the design. When the first half of the pattern is complete, a reverse tracing can be made to create the mirror reflection of the artwork.

Worked from a central line, the mirror-image pattern creates two identical sides to the design that are reflections of each other.

You can use any of the basic design shapes to create a mirror-image design: S-curves and C-curves, line designs, and triangular designs all work well. For example, making a mirror-image design from a triangular pattern allows you to use the larger design in one area of the structure and accent it with the single triangle designs in other areas.

Centerpiece designs also fall within the mirror-image category. These classic patterns, which include shell designs, vases, and garlands, are often used as accents on highboys and other pieces of furniture.

Since the mirror image is so obviously worked from a central line, a cameo pattern is sometimes added at the line to break the reflection. An example is the three-leaf cameo added below the ring in the design on the facing page.

To empasize the vertical lift of a piece, place the mirror image along the central line of the form. This placement works well for furniture designs that include tall doors or long, vertical panels. A mirror-image design may also be placed along the horizontal lines of the furniture form. Repeating a mirror-image pattern from drawer to drawer on a highboy can visually expand the width of the form while emphasizing the drawer work.

## MIRROR-IMAGE PLACEMENT

*Mirror images may be placed from a horizontal centerline to emphasize the height of the furniture (left), or they may be worked from a vertical centerline to emphasize the furniture's width (right).*

TRIPLE-LEAF ACANTHUS WITH RING

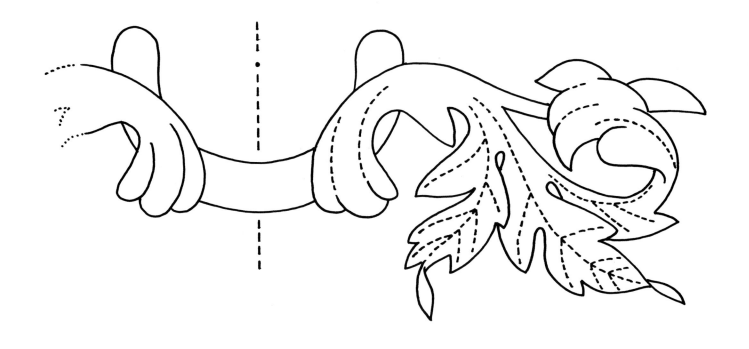

OPEN-CENTER HALF RING

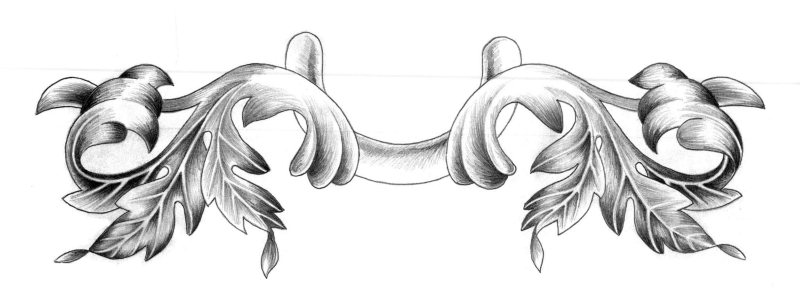

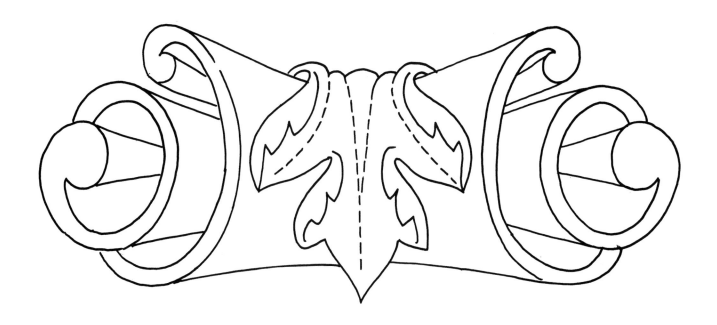

LEAF AND SCROLL

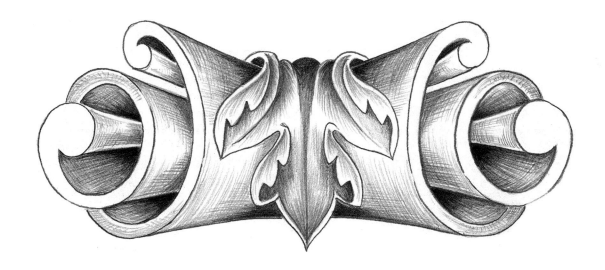

VICTORY-WREATH CENTERPIECE

CAPITAL COLUMN

QUEEN'S-CROWN LEAVES

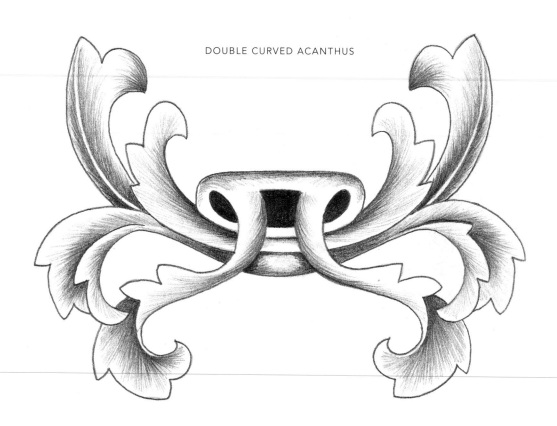

DOUBLE CURVED ACANTHUS

INTERLOCKED CRADLE HEARTS

BISHOP'S-SQUARE LEAVES

ROYAL-RIBBON LEAVES

SPLIT SCROLL AND ACANTHUS

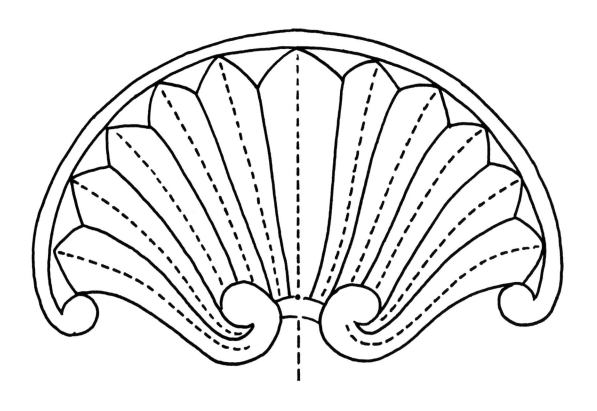

CLASSIC SHELL

SMALL HEART

LARGE HEART

LAUREL GARLAND

CORNERS AND CURLS

LILAC AND POPPY COMPOTE

WICKER BASKET

WINE-CHEST CORNICE

HIGHBOY SHELL

ROSE AND LAUREL SPRAY

CLASSIC CORNICE

OPEN-ROSE URN

# 8

# FREE-FORM DESIGNS

While many patterns are used to accent and complement the furniture on which they are placed, free-form designs are typically created to tell a story, either about the elements contained in the design or about the intended user of the piece. Storytelling through artwork is one of the oldest forms of expression.

Drama, emotion, and intrigue can all be found in a free-form design. The brier-patch rabbit shown below scurries through the grass, his body in full motion. From where has he come and where is he going?

The hunting falcon (see pp. 146-147) has been unhooded by his trainer, yet he is still tethered to the branch. He waits, tense and with wing feathers ruffled for his final release to the hunt. The traditional eagle and flag (see p. 152) shows another majestic bird in a free-form design. The eagle is shown proudly displaying his long wingspan. His head and chest curl over the flag in a protective posture, his expression one of determination. The feelings of strength, courage, and protectiveness are quickly identified by the viewer in this patriotic pattern.

The human face is blended with nature to create the North Wind image.

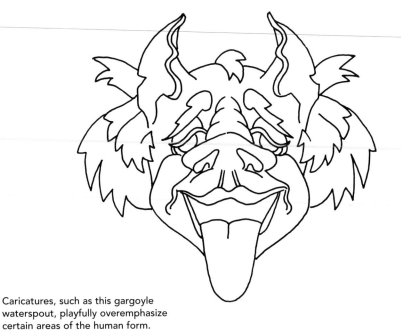

Caricatures, such as this gargoyle waterspout, playfully overemphasize certain areas of the human form.

Carvers and wood burners sometimes create fantasy patterns within the free-form design category. For example, North Wind designs are traditionally used to blend mankind and nature, as seen with the addition of spiraling horns and the leaf wreath to the ram's-horn North Wind at left. Artists occasionally poke fun at the human situation by creating caricatures that overemphasize certain human features, as shown in the drawing of the gargoyle waterspout below. Dragons and other mythical creatures may be used to show feelings of anger and power (see the drawing on the facing page).

A good way to place a free-form design onto the wood element is to use a bottom line of the pattern that corresponds to a bottom line of the wood. For example, the ground line under the rabbit on p. 141 makes a perfect reference line. Alternatively, the design can be contained within a border design as a square, rectangular, or circular shape and be transferred to the wood element as that shape (see, for example, the lion-corner pattern on pp. 144-145).

At the end of this chapter you'll find a number of cameos, beaded-line endings, and two complete alphabets, which can be used to accent and complement many of the designs found throughout this book. Cameos may be used to highlight selected areas of the wood element, such as keyholes, table legs, and the corners of a panel door, or to break up a long beaded line at the center point. Beaded-line endings add an interesting detail at the end of a raised line, say, on the apron of a Federal card table. And letters, in the form of initials, names, sayings, and so forth, can be used to personalize your design work and to commemorate special events.

ANTIQUE SCROLL DRAGON

LION CORNER

HUNTING FALCON

BRIER-PATCH RABBIT

RAM'S-HORN NORTH WIND

GARGOYLE WATERSPOUTS

TRADITIONAL EAGLE AND FLAG

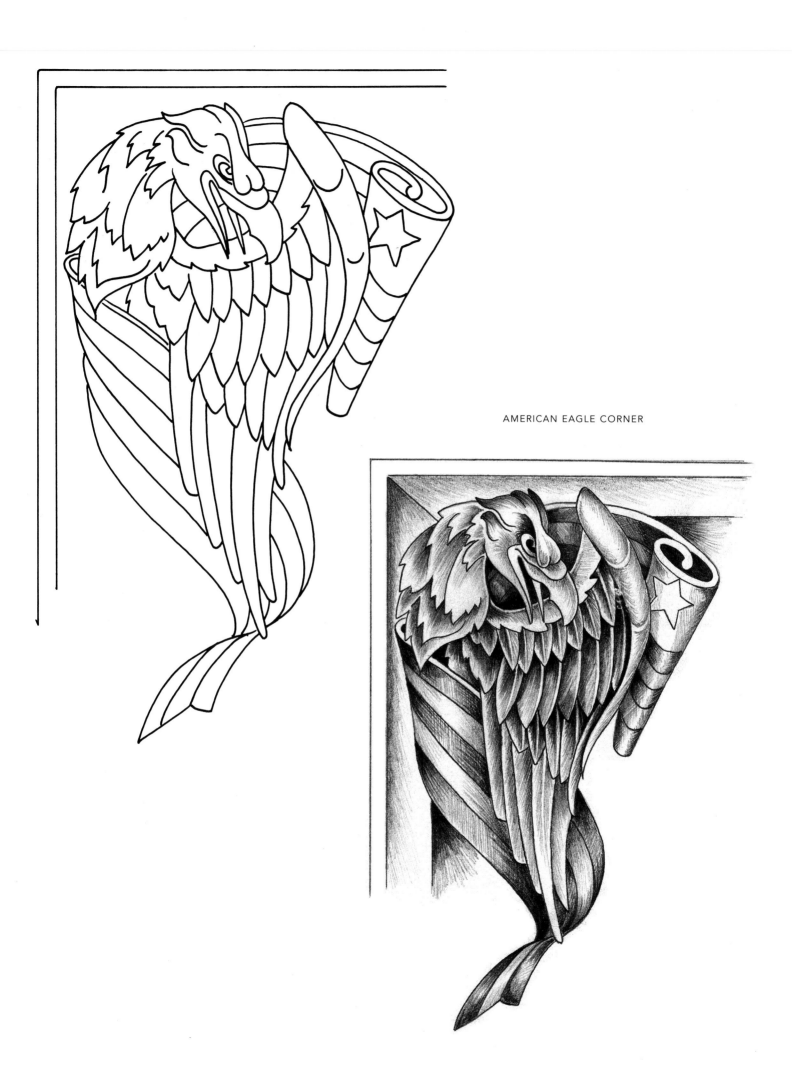

AMERICAN EAGLE CORNER

STARS AND BANNERS

BELLFLOWER CAMEO

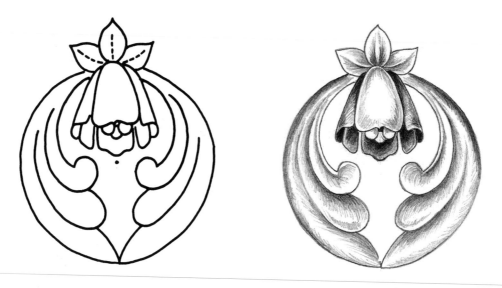

BELLFLOWER RING

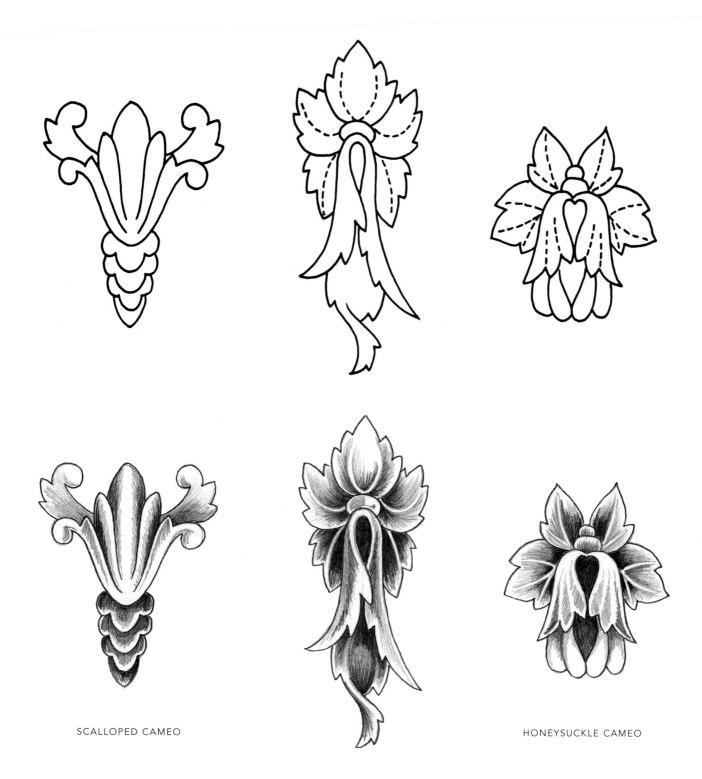

SCALLOPED CAMEO

SERRATED FLORAL CAMEO

HONEYSUCKLE CAMEO

CURLED-LEAF ACCENT

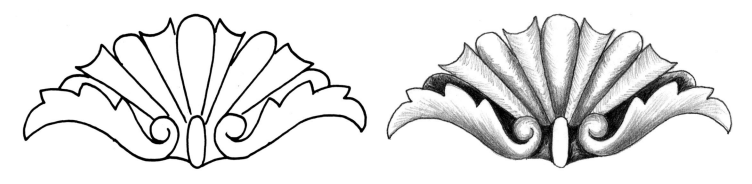

SHELL CAMEO

SIMPLE ROSE CAMEO

PETALED CORNER ACCENT

CIRCULAR LEAF ACCENT

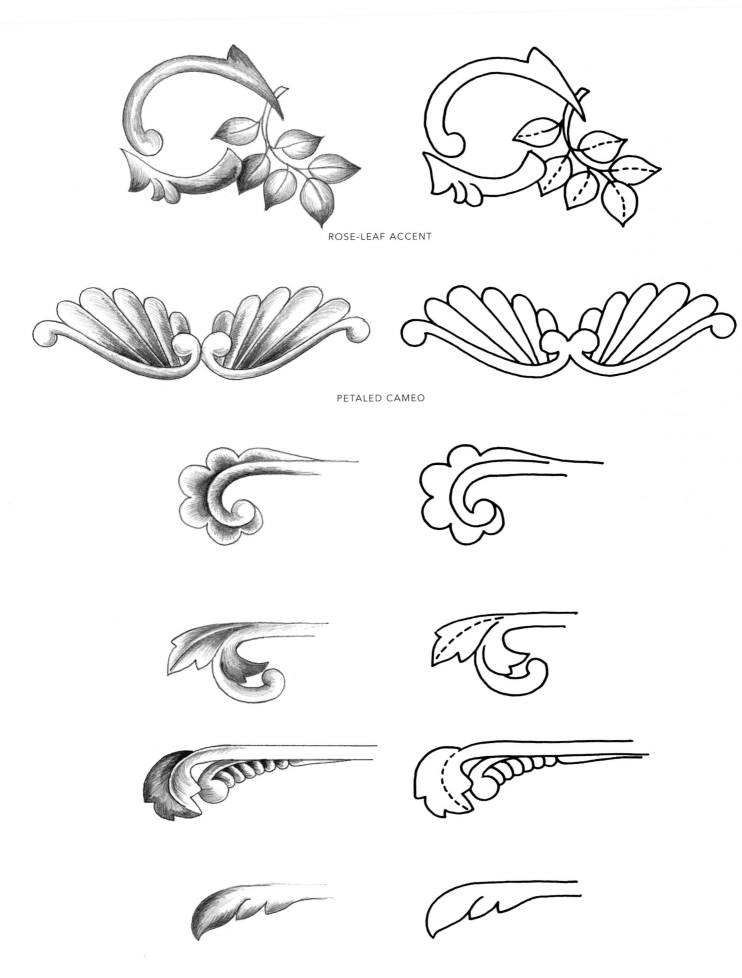

ROSE-LEAF ACCENT

PETALED CAMEO

BEADED-LINE ENDINGS

ABCD
EFGH
IJK
LMN

ROUND-SERIF ALPHABET

ROUND-SERIF ALPHABET

LEAF-CIRCLE MONOGRAM

LEAF-OVAL FERN

SCROLL-SCRIPT ALPHABET

STENCIL ROSE

# PLANNING & PLACEMENT

Deciding which pattern you wish to carve is just the beginning of the process that leads to picking up your carving knifes. You need to think about how the design will lie upon the wood and how it will affect the look of the furniture. This chapter considers the visual weight and the implied weight of the pattern and explains how to balance the two when placing the pattern on the wood. Also discussed is how to size a design to fit its area with the use of margins and air space.

Once you've sized the pattern, it's a good idea to test it on paper. Testing the pattern allows you to judge the overall effect of the carving on the furniture and make any adjustments before work begins. This chapter concludes with some ideas on how to move your chosen design onto paper and then transfer that paper pattern to the wood.

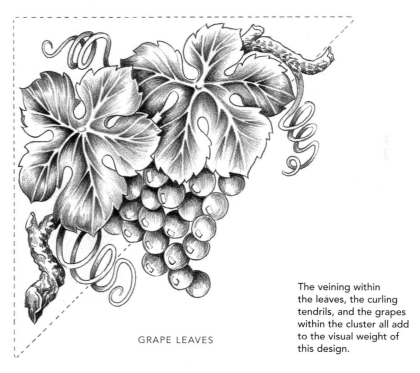

GRAPE LEAVES

The veining within the leaves, the curling tendrils, and the grapes within the cluster all add to the visual weight of this design.

## VISUAL WEIGHT AND IMPLIED WEIGHT

Design work has two types of weight: visual weight and implied weight. When choosing a pattern to enhance a wood form, you need to consider both.

### Visual Weight

Visual weight is determined by the space that the design occupies, the mass of the individual units within the design, the detail within each unit, and the air space that is captured by the pattern.

The grape-leaf design at top right fills its given space, reaching all the boundaries of the basic triangle. It is created with three massive units—two leaves and one cluster of grapes—each of which is highly detailed with either veining or individual grapes within the cluster. There is very little background within the design; what there is, is broken into very small areas. This pattern would be considered a visually heavy design.

Using a negative-image design, with the background darkened to show the amount of air space contained in the pattern, can help you determine the visual weight of a design.

WILD ROSE

STRAWBERRY

The wild-rose design at top left also fills its given space, yet it seems simply to *be* within its area rather than *be contained* within the space as does the grape-leaf pattern. The wild-rose pattern is created with six units—five leaf groups and one cluster of flowers. Since the design units are small in area, each contains finer details than the grape leaves. The wild-rose pattern contains much more air space than the grape-leaf design—nearly one-half of the basic triangle shape is background work. Such a design would be considered a medium-weight enhancement.

The strawberry design at bottom left is a lightweight design. It seems to have little relationship to the space it occupies. The four units within the design—three leaves and one berry cluster—are seen quite separately as individual units, each self-contained. As with the wild rose, the small units will accept finer and lighter detailing. More than one-half of the triangle area is air space, and it is accented by the long, sweeping lines of the stems. Even the added strawberry runner floats on a cushion of air.

## Implied Weight

Whereas the visual weight of the design is created by the artist, the implied weight is inferred by the viewer. The viewer uses that knowledge to judge the appropriateness of the design. The grape-leaf design represents one small part of the grapevine, a massive plant that can reach to the very canopy of the tree or trellis that it uses for its natural support. Eventually, the grapevine can overtake the trellis, and the base trunk of an old grapevine can easily reach 5 in. to 6 in. in width.

By contrast, the wild rose is a shrub that might reach 10 ft. to 12 ft. in height and up to 15 ft. in width. It has long, sweeping branches that arch down toward the ground. When in full bloom it seems almost to droop with the weight of its own flowers. What hardwood stems the wild rose has are hidden within the depths of the plant. This is a self-supporting plant, yet if grown in an upright position, it would need a trellis to hold its branches.

Finally, the strawberry is a perennial plant that reaches only 8 in. to 10 in. in height. Each year it dies back to the ground, preserving only a few leaves to begin its new growth in the spring. This plant is small and fragile in comparison to the grapevine or the wild rose.

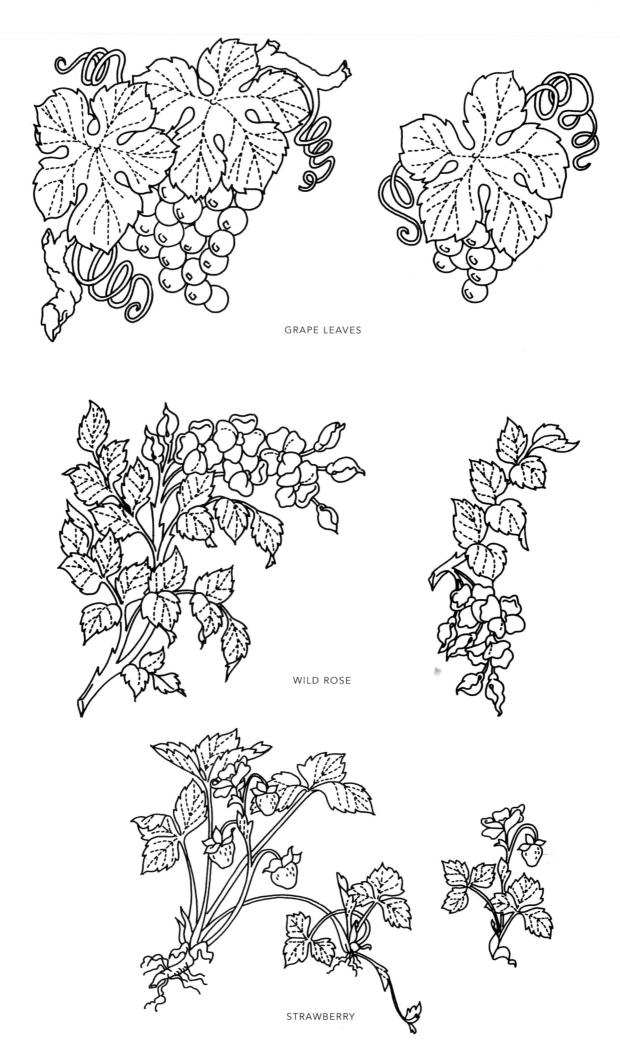

GRAPE LEAVES

WILD ROSE

STRAWBERRY

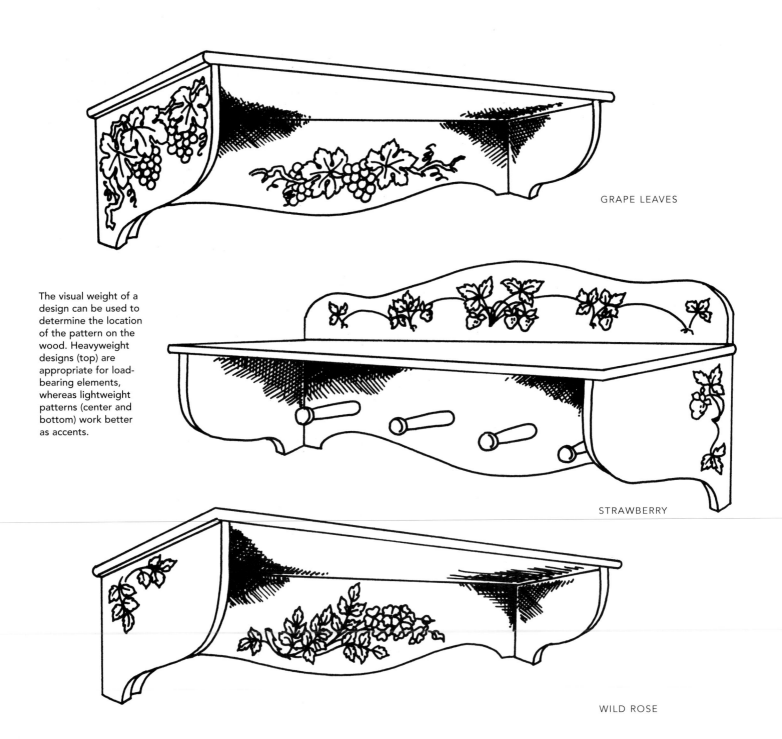

GRAPE LEAVES

The visual weight of a design can be used to determine the location of the pattern on the wood. Heavyweight designs (top) are appropriate for load-bearing elements, whereas lightweight patterns (center and bottom) work better as accents.

STRAWBERRY

WILD ROSE

When choosing which design to use on a wood element and where to use it, you need to balance the visual weight and the implied weight. On a simple wall-mounted bookshelf (see the drawings above), the grape-leaf design is visually strong enough and heavy enough to be used on the shelf supports. Just as the grapevine is strong enough to create its own trellis, its design will be strong enough to hold the weight of the books on the shelf.

The wild rose, though self-supporting, cannot support the weight of the books and should not be used on a main, load-bearing member of the shelf (except as a small accent). This design would be more appropriate on the lower back board, which adds stability to the form yet carries very little of the load of the shelf.

Finally, the small and fragile strawberry plant would be an excellent accent for an upper back board. Here it can reach for the air, resting on the shelf, without any weight from the books.

Using a large pattern with a narrow margin or a small pattern with a wide margin creates an unbalanced effect.

## MARGINS AND AIR SPACE

Design work needs to fit the form on which it is used. If the pattern is too large or overworked, it will overpower the piece and make it appear heavy and visually oppressive (see the drawing at left above). If the pattern is too small and isolated, it can become lost and insignificant (see the drawing at right above). With the careful use of margins and air space throughout the design, both situations can easily be avoided.

When artists place a painting or a print in a frame, they often surround the artwork with a mat. The mat provides an air space or visual pause between the work created in the painting and the wood frame. The mat allows the viewer to explore the painting and then to place it within the boundaries of the frame; it unites the two individual elements that complete the final picture.

You can use this same principle when placing a pattern on a wooden form: Creating an air space between the design work and the edge of the element has the same effect as using a mat around an art print. By using a carefully measured distance between the edge of the wood and the edge of the pattern, you can create a visual margin that allows the viewer's eye to make the transition between the pattern and the form (see the drawing below). Repeating this visual margin wherever the pattern is used provides continuity throughout the final form of the furniture.

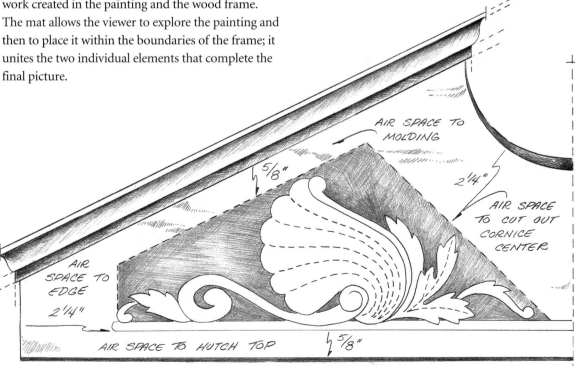

Allowing an equal margin at the top and bottom of the pattern and an equal margin at the sides centers the design within the space.

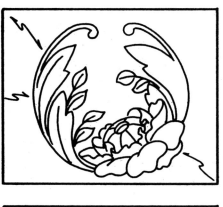

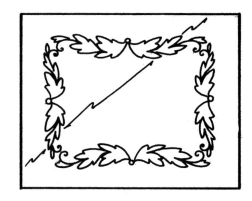

Different-shaped patterns require different treatment when sizing the design and the margin.

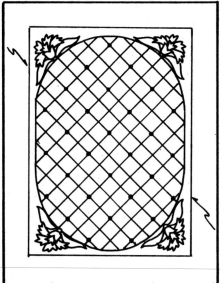

Make sure to choose a margin that is in proportion to the wood element on which it is used. As a general rule, I make the margins about one-eighth of the measurement of the wood element. For example, on a 16-in.-wide door panel I'd use margins about 2 in. wide around the outside edge, to give a pattern area approximately 12 in. wide.

Some patterns create their own margins and air space. Using a circular pattern on a square wood element automatically allows for uncarved or unpainted areas at each corner (as in the poppy circle in the drawing at top left). In this situation, you can bring a pattern close to the edges of the panel using a narrow margin along the sides. When using a square or rectangular pattern based on a linear design (see the drawing at top right), not only will there be margins around the outer edge but also air space within the design work. If you fill in the rectangular design with a quilting pattern (see the drawing at bottom left), the only air space for the design will be the margins that you allow. Mirror images and free-form designs tend to contain extra air space because they do not use controlled or static boundaries (see the drawing at bottom right).

The open areas and carved areas interblend within the pattern. With this style of pattern the margins are established from the individual units of the design.

If the margin around the pattern is more than one-third to one-half the width of the wood element, the design will be overpowered by the furniture. Consider enlarging the design to a more reasonable size, repeating the pattern in a mirror image to double its size, or adding a border or line accent to extend its given area. If, on the other hand, the pattern touches any edge of the wood element or seems to be crowded within the boundaries of the structure, you might wish to reduce the size of the pattern.

## TESTING THE PATTERN

Just as "measure twice and cut once" is a fundamental rule for carpenters and cabinetmakers, "test the pattern before you begin" should be the watchword for all wood carvers, wood burners, and wood painters. Making a simple test pattern on paper of the completed piece of furniture with the pattern in position can save hours of needless correction work.

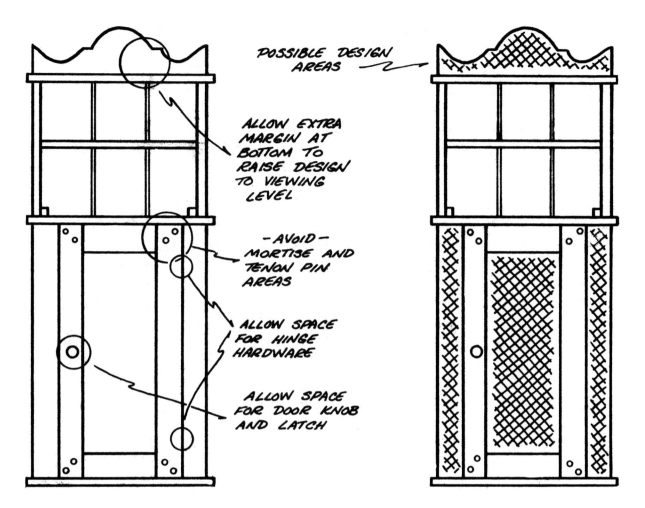

POSSIBLE DESIGN AREAS

ALLOW EXTRA MARGIN AT BOTTOM TO RAISE DESIGN TO VIEWING LEVEL

—AVOID—
MORTISE AND TENON PIN AREAS

ALLOW SPACE FOR HINGE HARDWARE

ALLOW SPACE FOR DOOR KNOB AND LATCH

Planning the location of the pattern work on the completed piece of furniture is a critical part of the design process.

When making a test pattern, keep both the wood form and the pattern in correct proportion to each other. Allow for all margins and air spaces that will be needed to fit the pattern to the piece (see the drawings above). Check the final test draft for continuity and for visual impact.

There are times when you may want to accent a wood form that has already been completed, as when you're adding a painted design to refinished furniture. In this case, sample patterns can be made and taped or tacked directly onto the piece before work begins. As with the test draft on paper, the pattern may then be viewed and any corrections in the design can be made before work begins. By using the test patterns, any changes that need to be made can be planned in advance.

As you work on the test pattern, keep in mind the following questions:

• What impacts the viewer first, the pattern and design work or the wood form of the furniture?

If the pattern work is prominent, scale it back to avoid overpowering the form. If, on the other hand,

the pattern work is scattered in small, indistinct areas throughout the form, you may want to rework it so the designs do not become isolated on the piece.

• Does one area of the test draft seem heavier or lighter with pattern work than other areas?

For example, if there is a concentration of design work on the door panels of a hutch, it might be better balanced by adding a design to the drawers.

• Does the pattern work complement both the style of the furniture and its final use?

If the pattern is a traditional heavy-leaf pattern, it may not be appropriate for a country-style blanket chest. Conversely, a pattern design of country geese might be better replaced with a traditional scroll or shell for use on a glassware hutch in a formal dining room.

• Does the pattern work have the visual weight to support or accentuate its given wood element?

If the pattern is appropriate in size to the area but seems too heavy visually, it can overpower the element

Once the test pattern has been completed on paper and any adjustments have been made, the design is ready to be transferred to the wood.

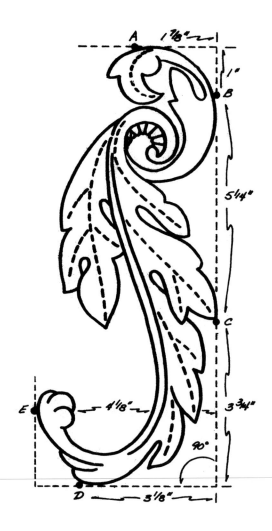

on which it is placed. If the pattern is appropriate in size but visually too light in weight, it can create a feeling that the design will be crushed by the wood form.

• Does the pattern work interfere with the final use of the wood form?

If the pattern extends from the back rail of a chair to its arm rests, the finished carving might be uncomfortable for the user. If the pattern extends to any edges, as along a drawer front, the work can easily be damaged with use.

• When the furniture is completed where will it most likely be displayed?

If in your original test plan you have included design work that will be hidden by a wall, such as carvings on the sides of a corner cupboard, this work will be lost when the piece is placed in its final position. If a desk will be freestanding in an office with a visitor's chair in front of it, the piece may need accent work on both the drawer side and on the back side so the carving can be seen both by the person sitting at the desk and by the visitor.

• Does the pattern work allow areas for any hardware that may be required on the furniture?

If a dresser drawer will require two drawer handles, you'll need to leave unaccented areas in the pattern for their placement.

• Does the pattern conflict with any features of the construction of the woodworking?

If the corners or edges of the form are constructed with decorative joinery techniques (such as dovetails), the pattern should not hide or disguise the work. If the pattern work does not allow enough margin or air space around the design, it may encroach upon edge details inherent in the form.

• Does the pattern invite the viewer to interact with the finished project.

If the pattern is well placed, it will focus the eye of the user on doors and drawers that ask to be opened. If the accents are well designed, they will encourage the user to touch the depths of the carving or feel the texture of the wood burning.

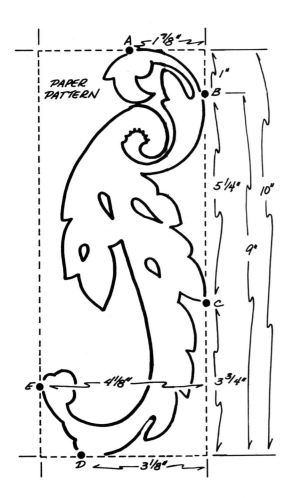

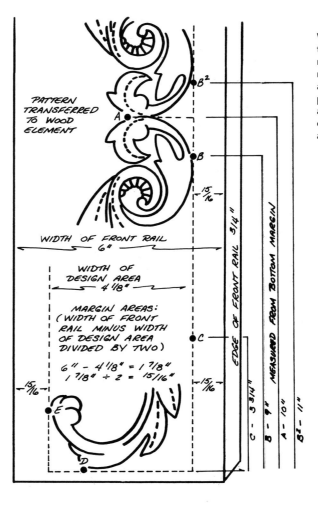

When transferring the pattern, all register marks and margin allowances are made on the paper pattern, and then repeated on the wood for accurate placement.

## TRANSFERRING THE PATTERN TO PAPER

Once you've chosen and tested the design that you wish to carve, burn, or paint, you'll need to make a copy of the pattern on a sheet of paper. There are several ways to trace a pattern easily and accurately without damaging the original pattern.

The simplest way to copy a pattern is to use a sheet of tracing paper; tracing velum and "onion-skin" typing paper both work well. Use very light pressure on the tracing pencil. Pressing too heavily will leave an impression from the pencil point in the original design. If you use a marker to trace the pattern, first test the marker on the tracing paper to make sure that the ink will not bleed through onto the original.

The pattern that you have chosen will often be used several times on a piece of furniture, both as it was originally traced and as a reverse copy. Onion-skin typing paper, although excellent for lifting the pattern, does not survive repeated tracing without tearing along the pencil lines. You'll need to make a new copy onto heavier paper, or make several copies using the onion skin.

A quick and easy way to transfer a pattern to a new piece of paper is to tape the pattern to the glass of a sunny window. Place a sheet of paper over the pattern and tape it into place. The light coming through the window will allow you to clearly see and trace the design. To reverse the pattern, simply tape the original design to the window with the pattern facing away from you.

To turn a pattern into a mirror image, trace the pattern onto one-half of a large sheet of paper. Fold the paper in half so that the fold line falls along what will become the centerline of the mirror image. Place the design with the sketch against the window and the clean half of the paper facing you. When you have traced the design and opened the paper, the sketch work and the tracing will be opposing, aligned, and ready for use. Symmetrical designs are more accurately created by sketching one-half of the pattern and then tracing the second half in reverse.

Another way to transfer the pattern is to use a light-box. You can make a lightbox with a piece of safety glass, several books, and a clip-on light or flashlight. Prop the back end of the glass evenly on two stacks of books to raise it 4 in. or 5 in. off the table. Place the light, facing toward the front edge of the glass, between the book stacks (see the drawing below). Turn off the room lights. Put the original pattern on top of the glass and cover it with a clean sheet of paper. The light from the clip-on light, just as the light from a sunny window, will allow you to see the pattern lines and make it easy to trace a copy onto the new sheet of paper.

Once you have experienced the convenience of using a lightbox, you may wish to add one to your design equipment. Lightboxes in various sizes, from desk models to freestanding table models, can be purchased through art-supply catalogs and office-supply stores. You can also make your own lightbox in your wood-shop using lamp parts that are available in woodworking catalogs and glass that can be purchased at your local hardware store.

It often happens that the pattern you wish to use does not fit the shape of your workpiece. For example, you may be looking for a corner pattern but the design you like is a straight line. The solution is to modify the pattern to fit your work. Make several copies of the pattern and then cut the design into small units: groups of leaves, clusters of flowers, and segments of ribbon or scrollwork. These smaller groups can then be arranged into the shape of your work, taped into their final position, and retraced to create your own arrangement (see the drawing on the facing page).

If the pattern you want to use is too small or too big, you can enlarge or reduce it on a photocopying machine. Using photocopies allows you to try several different sizes of the pattern without having to spend hours redrawing the pattern yourself. You can also use a pantograph to reproduce a design in any size. This simple device can be found for sale in many wood-working catalogs and is a wonderful addition to your design equipment.

## TRANSFERRING THE PATTERN TO WOOD

Once the pattern has been traced onto working sheets of paper, you are ready to transfer it to the wood. The easiest way to transfer the design is to use typing carbon paper, which leaves a clean dark line that will not accidentally rub off. Working with carbon paper is an effective method when you are making only a few copies of the design, but the carbon paper will not with-stand repeated use without tearing. When using carbon paper, be careful to trace as accurately as possible, since the lines can only be removed from the wood complete-ly either by carving or by sanding them out.

A second quick way to trace the pattern onto wood is to blacken the back of the pattern paper with a soft lead pencil. Be sure to cover the area completely with the pencil. Now position the pattern with the black-ened surface against the wood and trace over the design. As with carbon paper, this method is only good for a few copies before the pattern paper becomes too worn. However, it does avoid the problem of

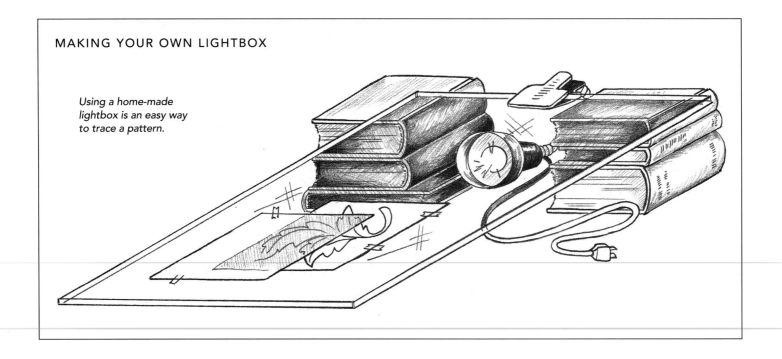

### MAKING YOUR OWN LIGHTBOX

*Using a home-made lightbox is an easy way to trace a pattern.*

## MODIFYING A PATTERN

You can create your own pattern or adjust the shape of an existing pattern by making several copies of different designs, cutting them apart, and then rearranging them into a new design.

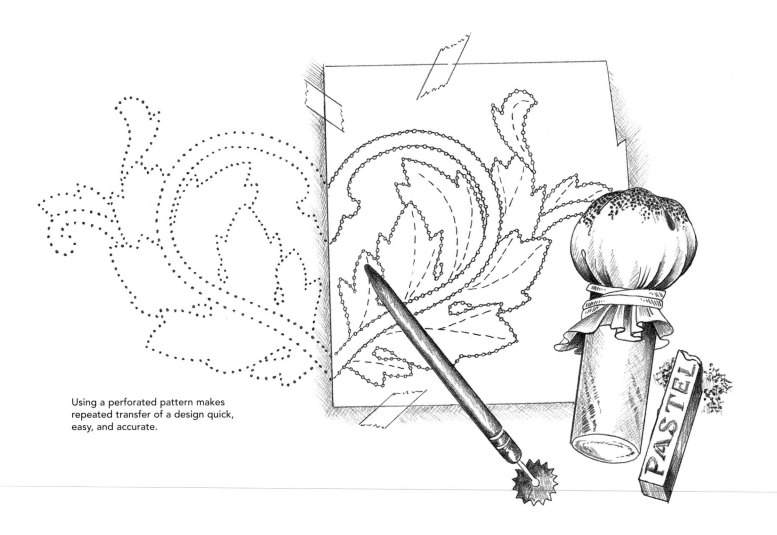

Using a perforated pattern makes repeated transfer of a design quick, easy, and accurate.

working with layers of paper, and the pencil marks that are made on the wood can be removed with an eraser. Once the pattern has been transferred, the pencil lines on the wood can be darkened by going over them again with the pencil.

When working on a dark-colored surface, regular carbon-paper tracing lines may not show well enough to work with easily. You can buy colored carbon paper from sewing stores and fabric shops, or rub white chalk across a rough-toothed paper to make an excellent tracing paper with light-colored lines.

To transfer large patterns to wood, metal, or painted surfaces, use sheets of newspaper instead of carbon paper. The newsprint ink will become a finely dotted line from which you can work. Any newsprint that is left after the work has been completed may be removed with a pencil eraser on wood or with a window-cleaner solution on painted and metal surfaces.

If you intend to use the same design over and over again, consider making a perforated pattern to save time over hand tracing (see the drawing above). Place the pattern to be used over a thick layer of newspaper.

Using a tracing wheel (available from fabric stores), firmly and slowly roll over all of the design lines. Lightly sand the back of the pattern paper with fine sandpaper to open all of the holes. Tape the pattern into place on the project and dust lightly with carbon dust for a dark tracing line or with chalk or talcum powder for a light-colored line.

With patterns that you know you'll use again and again, another way to save time is to make a template out of lightweight cardboard. Trace the pattern onto the cardboard, and then cut it out (use an X-acto knife to cut the inside lines). To use the template, place it on the workpiece and glide a pencil around the outside edge and through the inside cutouts. To keep the template from sliding, glue a piece of fine sandpaper to the template on the side of the design that will contact the work.

## Sources for Design Ideas

The patterns presented in this book should give you enough ideas to keep you carving, burning, or painting for many years to come. But if you're looking for new ideas, you might consider lifting designs from antique furniture, old gravestones, or even wallpaper.

Lifting a design from an antique piece of furniture can be difficult since you don't want to damage or mark the wood during the tracing process. To protect the piece, tape the pattern paper over the design work and use the flat edge of a soft pencil to cover the paper with graphite. As the pencil flat hits an edge of the design it will leave a darker mark (see the drawing above). The darker lines on the pattern paper can then be transferred to a new sheet of paper.

Sometimes the design that you wish to copy is too deeply carved to lift with a graphite rubbing. In this case, try taping a sheet of stiff tracing paper over the work. Use your finger to press the paper into the carving, causing the paper to crinkle and crease. The lines created by this pressing process will become your pattern.

Many old gravestones from the 1700s and 1800s have beautifully carved relief designs. To lift a design from a gravestone, you'll need a sheet of lightweight paper that completely covers the stone, a dabbing stick, and some carbon dust. To make a dabbing stick, first cover one end of a short piece of 1-in. dowel with a large wrap of cotton. Then place a piece of soft fabric, such

as T-shirt material, over the cotton wrap and secure it to the dowel with cord or rubber bands (see the drawing on the facing page). This will create a firm cotton-stuffed ball of fabric with a handle. Carbon dust can be obtained at an art-supply store, or you can make your own rubbing dust by grinding up soft pastel sticks. With the lightweight paper secured to the stone, pat the dabbing stick with dust, gently tap off any excess, and then rub the cotton-ball area over the design on the stone. Just as the flat of the pencil will leave darker marks on the paper where it contacts the relief, so will the rubbing dust. Work from the top of the stone down so that the excess dust does not obscure your work.

There are many other sources for design ideas. Wallpaper and fabric prints offer ideas on small repetitive patterns. Children's coloring books are a good source for simple shapes and childhood themes. Books on classic architecture provide ideas for corner patterns, panel designs, and scrollwork. Keep a file of any designs that catch your interest, and you'll have a ready reference at your fingertips as you plan new work.

# INDEX OF PATTERNS

**PUBLISHER**
James P. Chiavelli

**ACQUISITIONS EDITOR**
Rick Peters

**PUBLISHING COORDINATOR**
Joanne Renna

**EDITOR**
Peter Chapman

**DESIGNER/LAYOUT ARTIST**
Carol Singer

**PHOTOGRAPHERS**
Boyd Hagen *(pgs. 1, 170)*
Scott Phillips *(all others)*

**TYPEFACE**
Minion

**PAPER**
70-lb. Patina Matte

**PRINTER**
R.R. Donnelley, Willard, Ohio